WRITE!

Foundations and Models for Proficiency

Curriculum Associates

FOR THE STUDENT

WRITE! gives you the tools to be a better writer. You'll enjoy writing more, and you may even improve your writing scores!

FOUNDATIONS

In Part I, you'll think about and practice grammar, usage, and mechanics skills. You'll also study models of various kinds of writing, and you'll do some writing of your own!

MODELS

In Part II, you'll use what you've learned in Part I as you study models of several different forms of writing. For each form of writing, you will:

- see prompts and writing models.
- read partner and teacher comments on writing.
- correct errors in writing models.
- learn about rubrics, which are used to score writing.
- score some writing models on your own.
- do your own writing, with tips for help.
- work with a partner to score and improve your writing.
- make connections between writing and other parts of your life.

So, let's start to *WRITE!*

Acknowledgments

Product Development

Dale Lyle *Project Editor*

Joan Krensky *Project Editor*

Joan Talmadge *Project Editor*

Jo Pitkin *Writer*

Barbara Donovan *Writer*

J. A. Senn *Content Reviewer*

Design and Production

Susan Hawk *Designer/Illustrator*

Yvonne Cronin *Typesetter*

Photo/Illustration Credits

Pages 4, 6, 14, 16, 20, 26, 32, 34, 36, 40, 42, 46, 48, 50, 52, 54, 56, 60, 127 Clipart.com

Pages 8, 12, 18, 22, 24 ClipArt Explosion

Page 10 Yellowstone National Park Service

Page 28 Wild Animals/Corel

Page 30, 137 Library of Congress

Page 38 Southeast Asia/Corel

Page 44 National Image Gallery

Page 58 NASA

Page 135 photos.com

Page 144 NOAA Photo Library

ISBN 978-0-7609-2464-8

©2004—Curriculum Associates, LLC

North Billerica, MA 01862

TABLE OF CONTENTS

THINK ABOUT

Well-chosen **nouns** can add clarity and appeal to your writing.

A **noun** is word that names a person, place, thing, or idea.

A **concrete noun** names a person, place, or thing that can be seen or touched.

The following words are **concrete nouns:**

chef, woman, doctor, restaurant, lake, hospital, asparagus, geranium, periscope, figurine, crocodile.

An **abstract noun** names an idea, which cannot be seen or touched.

The following words are **abstract nouns:**

appetite, hunger, length, privacy, aroma, variation, enjoyment, pride, shame, ownership, intellect.

These **concrete nouns** name **people**:

waiter, customer, uncle, teacher, student, Stephen, Chef Child, Miss Lien, Dr. Ruiz.

These **concrete nouns** name **places**:

city, kitchen, desert, mall, Jim's Deli, North Carolina, Mount Fuji, Ocean Park, Greece.

These **concrete nouns** name **things**:

finger, menu, feather, knapsack, magazine, football, elephant, popcorn, pasta, Venus, Chinese food.

These **abstract nouns** name **ideas**:

skill, technique, fame, smell, taste, beauty, density, honor, dedication, enthusiasm, realism, Friday.

STUDY A MODEL

Read this help-wanted ad.

Concrete nouns are red, and abstract nouns are blue.

Help Wanted

Pizza Palace will open soon. The owner is now hiring cooks. Responsibilities include the preparation of sauce and dough and the invention of new recipes for special pizzas. The work is approximately 20 hours per week. Applicants should submit a resume. Prior experience is not necessary. Salary is negotiable. Your independence, creativity, and flexibility are desirable.

Contact Mr. D'Angelino at the restaurant

◀ ● ● In the first sentence, the concrete noun *Pizza Palace* names a particular place that you can see or touch. It is also a proper noun made up of two separate words that are capitalized.

◀ ● ● Notice that the words *experience* and *Salary* are abstract nouns. They name ideas that you cannot see or touch.

◀ ● ● Here, the concrete noun *Mr. D'Angelino* names a particular person, and *restaurant* names a particular place.

PRACTICE

A *Write each noun and label it C for concrete or A for abstract.*

1. their achievement
2. the chair
3. our assistant
4. her promotion
5. the editor
6. his intelligence
7. a desk
8. your ability
9. the printer
10. my recovery

B *Read each sentence. Write the concrete noun and the abstract noun.*

1. The new manager will start in October.
2. Our department attended the conference.
3. Can you get the attention of the editor-in-chief?
4. Call a technician for assistance.
5. Production of the paper is slow.
6. The artists displayed healthy competition.
7. This report shows that profits are up.
8. Mrs. Quantrel showed her appreciation.
9. All employees will get some extra vacation.
10. Available times will be posted on the board.

C *Read the paragraph. Write the 10 concrete nouns and the 9 abstract nouns. One concrete noun is used more than once.*

Tina works at the Thespian Theater. She answers the telephones, files papers, and handles reservations. Tina enjoys the arts, and she likes working in the busy environment. Tina also enjoys the challenge of photography. Her photos have been used at the theater as part of several promotions. Because of her knowledge, ability, and talent, Tina is a highly valued employee.

A **concrete noun** names a person, place, or thing that can be seen or touched. An **abstract noun** names an idea, which cannot be seen or touched.

WRITE

Write a help-wanted ad that might appear in your local newspaper. Remember to use both concrete and abstract nouns in your writing to make the job seem realistic.

Writing Tip

Remember that you can use **compound nouns** and **collective nouns** in your writing.

A **compound noun** is made up of more than one word (firefighter, New Jersey, self-knowledge).

A **collective noun** names a group of people, animals, or things (team, company, chorus, herd).

NOUN SUFFIXES

THINK ABOUT

Some nouns have special endings called **noun suffixes**.

Common Noun Suffixes

-ance	-ence	-ion	-ment
-ation	-ent	-ism	-ness
-dom	-er	-ist	-or
-ee	-ery	-ity	-ure

- The suffix *-ance* means "the act of, state of being." *acceptance, performance*
- The suffix *-ence* means "the act of, quality or state of." *occurrence, intelligence*
- The suffix *-ment* means "state of being, act of, result of." *enjoyment, pavement*
- The suffixes *-er* and *-or* mean "one who does something." *explorer, actor*
- The suffix *-ness* means "state or condition of." *happiness, fierceness*
- The suffix *-ity* means "state or quality of." *equality, productivity*

You can form a noun by adding a noun suffix to a verb or an adjective.

Verb		Noun Suffix		Noun
hibernate	+	ion	=	**hibernation**
appear	+	ance	=	**appearance**
swim	+	er	=	**swimmer**
improve	+	ment	=	**improvement**
fail	+	ure	=	**failure**

Adjective		Noun Suffix		Noun
curious	+	ity	=	**curiosity**
futile	+	ity	=	**futility**
fearless	+	ness	=	**fearlessness**
lovely	+	ness	=	**loveliness**

Notice that the spelling of some base words changes when a noun suffix is added.

imagine	+	ation	=	**imagination** (the *e* is dropped)
active	+	ity	=	**activity** (the *e* is dropped)
happy	+	ness	=	**happiness** (the *y* is changed to *i*)

STUDY A MODEL

Read the journal entry that Karen wrote about her first day at camp.

> *The nouns with noun suffixes are red.*

July 8

I arrived at Camp Woodland yesterday. The other campers and counselors seem friendly. In orientation we learned about camp activities. We will swim, make our own pottery, work on a camp sculpture, and take long hikes. A local environmentalist will raise our awareness of the surrounding area. The camp baker is supposed to be excellent, and my cabin is next to the dining hall! Our days are scheduled, but we have the freedom to do what we want at night. I'm looking forward to the next two weeks with great anticipation!

Note that the nouns *campers* and *counselors* are verbs with noun suffixes.

The nouns *environmentalist* and *awareness* are adjectives with noun suffixes.

The noun *freedom* is also an adjective, with the noun suffix *-dom.*

PRACTICE

A *Write the noun suffix in each noun.*

1. productivity
2. kingdom
3. preference
4. trickery
5. naturalist
6. sailor
7. kindness
8. improvement

B *Read each sentence. Use the noun suffix in parentheses to make the underlined verb or adjective a noun.*

1. The <u>hike</u> slowed at the top of Bull Hill. (er)
2. He enjoyed the <u>still</u> of the woods. (ness)
3. The steep trail required <u>endure</u>. (ance)
4. Reaching the top would be an <u>accomplish</u>. (ment)
5. Being a guide is a great <u>responsible</u>. (ity)
6. Our guide is a <u>special</u>. (ist)
7. Bring food, water, medical <u>inform</u>, and maps. (ation)
8. Follow the hike to its <u>complete</u>. (ion)

C *Read the paragraph. Write the 12 nouns that end with noun suffixes. Underline the suffixes.*

    Meriwether Lewis and William Clark were well-known explorers. President Thomas Jefferson asked them to lead an expedition to lands in the West. After their departure from St. Louis in May of 1804, Lewis and Clark and about fifty other travelers journeyed for more than two years. They walked, rode horses, and used boats for transportation. They hired a fur trader and his wife, Sacagawea, as guides and interpreters. The group experienced cold temperatures, exhaustion, and a lack of food. However, their trip was very successful. Their contribution was a better understanding of climate, geography, and plants and animals in the West. They also brought back important information about Native American cultures.

> Some nouns end with a **noun suffix,** such as *-ance, -ence, -er, -ity, -ment,* or *-ness.*

WRITE

Write a journal entry about an outdoor experience that you've had. Be careful to spell nouns with noun suffixes correctly.

Writing Tip

You can also add **suffixes** to **nouns** to form **adjectives.**

Noun	Suffix		Adjective
mountain	+ ous	=	mountainous
color	+ ful	=	colorful
person	+ al	=	personal
queen	+ ly	=	queenly

POSSESSIVE NOUNS

THINK ABOUT

A noun changes its form to show that it owns (or is closely connected to) something else. A **possessive noun** shows who or what owns something.

Add an apostrophe and an *s* (*'s*) to a singular noun to make it possessive.

Singular Nouns	Possessive Nouns
the toy belonging to the *dog*	the *dog's* toy
the mast of a *ship*	the *ship's* mast
the throw of the *pitcher*	the *pitcher's* throw
the dinner by *Chef Aron*	*Chef Aron's* dinner

Add an apostrophe and an *s* (*'s*) even if the singular noun ends in *s*.

Singular Nouns	Possessive Nouns
the home of *Walt Davis*	*Walt Davis's* home
the tires of the *bus*	the *bus's* tires
a role of an *actress*	an *actress's* role

Add only an apostrophe (') to a plural noun that ends in *s* to make it possessive.

Plural Nouns	Possessive Nouns
the caps of the *players*	the *players'* caps
the tents of the *nomads*	the *nomads'* tents
the mother of the *calves*	the *calves'* mother
the report of the *scientists*	the *scientists'* report
the songs by the *singers*	the *singers'* songs

Add an apostrophe and an *s* (*'s*) to a plural noun that does not end in *s*.

Plural Nouns	Possessive Nouns
the laughter of the *children*	the *children's* laughter
the choice of the *people*	the *people's* choice
the tails of the *mice*	the *mice's* tails
the trail of the *geese*	the *geese's* trail
the wool of the *sheep*	the *sheep's* wool

STUDY A MODEL

Read this passage from a sports article.

In the fourth inning of yesterday's game between the Hawks and the Lions, Ken Brown's solo homer put the Lions up by a run. After six innings' play, Tom Bonanno of the Hawks hit a line drive. Then Brett Starr smacked one right between the first and second basemen's gloves. The Lions' coach's decision to bring in a new pitcher was smart. With two on base, Juan Ramirez's pop-out did it. The Lions held a one-run lead until the bottom of the ninth. Then the shortstop's double, an outfielder's error, and the baserunners' speed won them the game.

The singular possessive nouns are red, and the plural possessive nouns are blue.

 Notice that the possessive nouns *yesterday's* and *Ken Brown's* are singular. They are formed by adding an apostrophe and an *s*.

 The possessive noun *innings'* is plural. It is formed by adding only an apostrophe.

The possessive noun *basemen's* is plural. It is formed by adding an apostrophe and an *s*.

 Because *Juan Ramirez's* is a singular possessive noun, an apostrophe and an *s* were added.

PRACTICE

A *Rewrite each phrase using a possessive noun.*

1. the property of a landlord
2. a solo by the soprano
3. the uniforms of the firefighters
4. the soft down of the geese
5. the sketches of the cartoonists
6. the review by the critic

B *Read the sentences. Write the 3 singular possessive nouns and the 4 plural possessive nouns.*

1. The announcer's booth was filled with laughter.
2. The quarterback's contract has been signed.
3. The women's field hockey team won the trophy.
4. Did Dana get this year's award?
5. The people's choice is clear.
6. The children's new playground will open Friday.
7. The boys' team lost in the playoffs.

C *Read the paragraph. Find and correct the 5 singular nouns and the 5 plural nouns that should be possessive.*

   Wilma Rudolph was one of Americas most famous athletes. Young Wilma had many serious childrens illnesses, including polio. This left the young girls leg weak and crooked. She wore a heavy leg brace for years. With her mothers help, however, she was able to walk again without a brace. As a teenager, Rudolph joined her schools basketball team. She played in the Tennessee High School Girls Championship. Later, as a member of the womens track team at Tennessee State University, Rudolph set records. Competing in the 1960 Olympic Games, she won three gold medals to the fans delight. One of the worlds fastest women, Rudolph gained peoples great admiration.

A **possessive noun** shows who or what owns something. To form a possessive: add 's to a singular noun, add ' to a plural noun that ends in s, add 's to a plural noun that does not end in s.

WRITE

Write a sports article about a real or imaginary athlete or athletic contest. Be careful to form possessive nouns correctly.

Writing Tips

- Don't confuse **plural nouns** with **possessive nouns**. Use possessive nouns only to show ownership:
  The athletes warm up. (no ownership)
  Here are the athletes' warm-up clothes.
- **Pronouns** also show possession: my, your, his, her, its, our, their; mine, yours, his, hers, its, ours, theirs.
  This is my book.   That is mine.
  Where is her pie?   Where is hers?

SUBJECT AND OBJECT PRONOUNS

THINK ABOUT

When you want to avoid repetition in your writing, you can use **personal pronouns** to take the place of nouns. The nouns replaced are called *antecedents*. The pronouns may be **subject pronouns** or **object pronouns**, depending on how you use them.

Subject Pronouns: *I, we, you, he, she, it, they*

Use a **subject pronoun** to take the place of a noun that is a **subject** in a sentence.

> *Kara* ate lunch. *She* ate lunch.
> *The players* celebrated. *They* celebrated.

When a subject pronoun is part of a **compound subject**, make sure the pronoun is in the correct **form** and in the correct **order**.

> *He* likes cats. *I* like cats.
> *He and I* like cats. (not *he and me* or *me and him* or *I and he*)

Use a **subject pronoun** to take the place of a noun that follows a **linking verb** such as *is, are, was, were,* or *will be.*

> The winner is *Patty.* The winner is *she.*

Object Pronouns: *me, us, you, him, her, it, them*

Use an **object pronoun** to take the place of a noun that is used as a **direct object, indirect object,** or the **object of a preposition** such as *above, after, around, at, before, behind, for, from, near, over, to, toward,* or *with.*

> **Direct Object:** The class elected *Jason.* The class elected *him.*
> **Indirect Object:** Hand *Ellie* the hammer. Hand *her* some nails, too.
> **Object of Preposition:** The neighbors depend on *Earl and Ella.* The neighbors depend on *them.*

When an object pronoun is part of a **compound object**, make sure the pronoun is in the correct **form** and in the correct **order**.

> Mom gave *him* a kitten. Mom gave *me* a kitten.
> Mom gave *him and me* a kitten. (not *he and I* or *me and him* or *him and I*)

Remember that a pronoun and its antecedent can be in different sentences.

> *Chris* worked all morning. *He* finished early.
> Sell the books to *Miss Lane* and her *student.* Give *them* a discount.

STUDY A MODEL

Read the note from Karen to Miya.

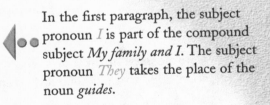

Subject pronouns are red, and object pronouns are blue.

Dear Miya,

My family and I arrived yestereday. Yellowstone is a huge park! The guides are helpful. They know a lot about the park's history, and one guide gave Dad and me some Yellowstone brochures.

This morning, Kerry told me an interesting fact. Bighorn sheep, elk, and buffalo live here. Wildlife interests her and me alike. Last night, she and I heard coyotes howling in the mountains behind us. What kind of animals are they? Maybe Kerry and I will take some photos.

Your friend,

Karen

In the first paragraph, the subject pronoun *I* is part of the compound subject *My family and I.* The subject pronoun *They* takes the place of the noun *guides.*

In the second paragraph, the object pronoun *me* is an indirect object.

The object pronouns *her* and *me* are part of a compound direct object, and the subject pronouns *she* and *I* are part of a compound subject. Note that the pronouns are stated in the correct order (not *me and her*).

The subject pronoun *they* follows the linking verb *are.*

PRACTICE

A *Label each pronoun S for subject or O for object.*

1. him *O*
2. they *S*
3. I *S*
4. her *O*
5. we *S*
6. us *O*
7. them *O*
8. she *S*
9. he *S*
10. me *O*

B *Read each sentence. Write the correct pronoun to complete the sentence.*

1. The cave's entrance loomed before (we, *us*).
2. The geologist cautioned (they, *them*) to be careful.
3. A guide handed flashlights to Jason, Kara, and (I, *me*).
4. An expert in caves is (he, *him*).
5. Jason and (*I*, me) went first into the darkness.
6. (*We*, Us) felt an icy blast of cold air.
7. Roberto handed his brother and (she, *her*) some gloves.
8. Kara said the blast hit (she, *her*) too.
9. Kara asked Jason and (*I*, me) to take the lead.
10. The twins and (they, *them*) went further in the cave.

C *Read the paragraph. Rewrite the paragraph, using the pronouns that correctly complete it.*

Alycia and Sean enjoy scuba diving. (*They*, Them) take lessons to learn how to breathe correctly. An instructor shows (they, *them*) the proper use of equipment. Both Alycia and Sean are strong swimmers, but the better swimmer is (*she*, her). Soon Mr. Champion will swim between her and (he, *him*) in a swimming pool. Then Alycia and (he, *him*) will do some practice dives. Finally, Mr. Champion will give Sean and (she, *her*) a certificate when they are ready for the open water.

A **subject pronoun** replaces a noun that is a subject in a sentence or that follows a linking verb.
An **object pronoun** replaces a direct or indirect object of a verb or follows a preposition.

WRITE

Write a note to a friend, family member, or classmate about a real or imaginary trip. Be sure to use subject and object pronouns correctly.

Writing Tip

You can make sure you are using the right form of a **pronoun** in a **compound subject** or **compound object** by using the pronoun alone in the sentence.

Incorrect: Ted and me made lunch.
Me made lunch. (doesn't sound right)

Correct: Ted and I made lunch.
I made lunch. (sounds right)

11

INTERROGATIVE AND RELATIVE PRONOUNS

THINK ABOUT

Use an **interrogative pronoun** to ask a question.

Interrogative Pronouns	Sentences
who	*Who* solved the mystery? (Use *who* as a subject.)
whom	*Whom* did they elect? (Use *whom* as a object.)
whose	*Whose* is this?
which	*Which* is the most difficult question?
what	*What* was their answer?

Use a **relative pronoun** to introduce a group of words that describes a noun or pronoun in a sentence.

Relative Pronouns	Sentences
	Do not use commas to set off a group of words that is *essential* to the meaning of the sentence.
who	The author *who* wrote this novel is clever.
whom	The actors *whom* we chose fit the roles perfectly.
whose	The girl *whose* hand was up asked the first question.
that	I chose the peach *that* was the ripest.
	Do use commas to set off a group of words that is *not essential* to the meaning of the sentence.
who	Kim, *who* loves cats, got a new kitten.
which	I passed the final exam, *which* lasted several hours.

STUDY A MODEL

Read the interview between fictional detective Sherlock Holmes and a robbery suspect.

Sherlock Holmes: What happened to the diamond necklace?

Red-haired Man: The woman who wore the necklace to the opera still has it.

Holmes: Who was your other accomplice?

Red-haired Man: My nephew. He made the appointment that got us into the mansion.

Holmes: Whose fingerprints are on the safe?

Red-haired Man: Those prints, which Watson discovered by mistake, belong to the person whose necklace was stolen.

The interrogative pronouns are red, and the relative pronouns are blue.

The relative pronoun *who* introduces the group of words *who wore the necklace to the opera*, which describes the word *woman*.

The interrogative pronoun *Who* introduces a question.

The relative pronoun *that* introduces a group of words that describes the word *appointment*.

The interrogative pronoun *Whose* introduces a question.

Which, set off by commas, introduces a group of words that describes the word *prints*.

Whose introduces a group of words that describes the word *person*. Within the group of words, *whose* describes the word *necklace*.

PRACTICE

A *Read each sentence. Write the pronoun and label it I for interrogative or R for relative.*

1. Who played the detective in the movie?
2. Which was the bestseller?
3. Is the villain the actor who is missing an arm?
4. The end, which revealed the solution, was a surprise.
5. Liam enjoys mysteries that have a happy ending.
6. What is the title of this author's recent thriller?

B *Write an interrogative pronoun or a relative pronoun to complete each sentence.*

1. ___(interrogative)___ made this counterfeit money?
2. We counted the bills, ___(relative)___ were nearly perfect copies.
3. ___(interrogative)___ did you call for help?
4. ___(interrogative)___ happens if a person spends counterfeit money?
5. The government has new techniques ___(relative)___ reveal counterfeit bills.
6. The shopper ___(relative)___ passed counterfeit tens was arrested.

C *Read the paragraph. Label each of the 7 underlined pronouns I for interrogative or R for relative.*

Who was Edgar Allan Poe? He was a 19th-century American writer who pioneered a popular type of literature. Poe's short story "The Murders in the Rue Morgue," which was published in 1841, was the first modern detective story. Poe was a writer whose eerie crime tales fascinated readers. Poe himself was the center of a mystery. In 1849, he collapsed on the street and was taken to a hospital. He died a few days later from a condition that included delusions. What actually caused Poe's death? Some believe he died as a result of substance abuse. Others believe he had a case of rabies, which can be transmitted by animal bites.

An **interrogative pronoun** (*who, whom, whose, which, what*) introduces a question. A **relative pronoun** (*who, whom, whose, which, that*) introduces a group of words that describes.

WRITE

Write an interview with a book, movie, or TV character. Be sure to use interrogative and relative pronouns correctly.

Writing Tip
- In writing, use the **relative pronoun which** to introduce a group of words that could be removed without changing the basic meaning of the sentence. Use **commas** to set off this **nonessential** group of words.

  The final clue, **which** was very subtle, cracked the case. (not essential, could be taken out)
- Use the **relative pronoun that** to introduce a group of words that is **essential** to the understanding of the sentence. Do not use commas.

  The team **that** cracked the case celebrated. (essential, necessary to know which team)

REFLEXIVE AND INTENSIVE PRONOUNS

The word *reflexive* means "bending back." A **reflexive pronoun** reflects the action of the verb back to the subject.

In the following sentence, both *she* and *herself* are involved in the action of the verb *bought*.

She bought *herself* a new computer.

A singular reflexive pronoun ends in *-self*.
A plural reflexive pronoun ends in *-selves*.

Singular	Plural
myself	ourselves
yourself	yourselves
himself, herself, itself	themselves

A reflexive pronoun can be used as a **direct object**, an **indirect object**, or the **object of a preposition**.

Direct Object: My cat cleans *itself*.
Indirect Object: Sira wrote *herself* a note.
Object of a Preposition: He told a story about *himself*.

Do not use a reflexive pronoun where a subject pronoun belongs.

Incorrect: Pat and *myself* played ball.
Correct: Pat and *I* played ball.

Do not use a reflexive pronoun where an object pronoun belongs.

Incorrect: Will you contact Luisa and *myself*?
Correct: Will you contact Luisa and *me*?

Do not use *hisself, themself, theirself, theirselves,* or *ourself*. These are not words.

An **intensive pronoun** is a reflexive pronoun that adds emphasis to a **subject**. An intensive pronoun usually, but not always, directly follows the subject. An intensive pronoun could be removed without changing the meaning of the sentence.

Have *you yourself* ever painted an entire house?
Roberto himself chose the geometry courses.
The *puppy itself* finished all the food.
Did *Shelly* write the report *herself*?
The *players* get all the credit *themselves*.

STUDY A MODEL

Read this passage from a build-your-own bicycle kit.

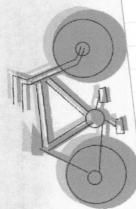

Build Your Own Bicycle

You yourself can build a bicycle! All you need are a few tools and our easy instructions. Soon, you will be pedaling yourself down the path to adventure.

The aluminum frame itself comes assembled. Customers attach the other parts by themselves. Whether you build a tricycle or a racing bike that Lance Armstrong himself might ride, all parts are guaranteed. Our company prides itself on fine craftsmanship!

The reflexive pronouns are red, and the intensive pronouns are blue.

The intensive pronoun *yourself* adds emphasis to the subject *you*, but *yourself* could be removed without changing the meaning of the sentence.

The reflexive pronoun *yourself* reflects back to the subject *you*.

The reflexive pronoun *themselves* is the object of the preposition *by* and reflects back to *Customers*. The words *Customers* and *themselves* refer to the same group of people.

PRACTICE

A *Read each sentence. Label the underlined pronoun R for reflexive or I for intensive.*

1. Tamika made <u>herself</u> a sweater.
2. She selected the colors and pattern <u>herself</u>.
3. Tamika and I taught <u>ourselves</u> how to knit.
4. Most of the stitches <u>themselves</u> were easy to learn.
5. The instruction sheet <u>itself</u> clearly explained the steps.
6. Would you knit <u>yourself</u> a pair of socks?

B *Read each sentence. Write the intensive pronoun and the subject that it emphasizes.*

1. Nara herself is an authority on native plants.
2. We must protect the environment ourselves.
3. I myself am a fervent chess player.
4. The workers achieved the breakthrough themselves.
5. She herself is the expert quoted in the newspaper.
6. Do you yourself receive a discount from the store?
7. The diplomats themselves expressed doubts.

C *Read the paragraph. Label each of the 5 underlined pronouns R for reflexive or I for intensive.*

William H. Jackson was a well-known photographer. In 1874, Jackson traveled to ancient Anasazi cliff dwellings in southwestern Colorado. Jackson and his photographic crew hauled large cameras up the steep cliffs of Mancos Canyon by <u>themselves</u>. Then Jackson <u>himself</u> made the first photographs of Mesa Verde. One apartment house, which stood by <u>itself</u> in a canyon wall, was four stories high. An 1876 exhibition of Jackson's large black-and-white photographs of the dwellings was a success. Today you <u>yourself</u> can view these photographs. They are displayed in the U.S. Department of the Interior in Washington, D.C. People still wonder how Native Americans built these impressive structures by <u>themselves</u>.

A **reflexive pronoun** (*myself, yourself, himself, herself, itself, ourselves, yourselves, themselves*) reflects action back to the subject it follows. An **intensive pronoun** adds emphasis to the subject it follows but does not change the meaning of the sentence.

WRITE

Write a paragraph giving instructions on how to do a project, sport, craft, or household chore. Use reflexive and intensive pronouns correctly.

Writing Tip

In your writing, you may also use **indefinite pronouns**. These take the place of nouns that are not clearly identified. Some indefinite pronouns are *someone, anyone, nobody, no one, nothing,* and *something*.

- No one knows the answer.
- Something is wrong with Clarisse.
- Will someone please call Mom tonight?

VERB TENSES

THINK ABOUT

Using the correct **tense** of **verbs** will tell readers exactly when something happens. Verbs express action or tell something about a subject. Verb tenses express time. You often use the *present*, *past*, and *future* tenses. Sometimes, however, you need to use **present perfect**, **past perfect**, or **future perfect tenses** to tell when something is happening.

- The **present perfect tense** refers to something that occurred at some indefinite time in the past or that began sometime in the past and continues in the present. To form the present perfect tense, combine the helping verb *has* or *have* with the *past participle*.

Present	Past	Past Participle
break	broke	broken
do	did	done
eat	ate	eaten
leave	left	left
make	made	made
ring	rang	rung
see	saw	seen
speak	spoke	spoken

Present Perfect Verbs in Sentences:
  Snow *has fallen* all day.
  We *have spoken* on the phone.

- The **past perfect tense** refers to something that happened in the past before a specific time or event in the past. To form the past perfect tense, combine the helping verb *had* with the *past participle*.

Past Participles: guessed, arrived
Past Perfect Verbs in Sentences:
  Mel *had guessed* what the gift was before he opened the box.
  Several guests *had arrived* before sunset.

- The **future perfect tense** refers to something that will be completed by a specific time or event in the future. To form the future perfect tense, combine the helping verb *will have* with the *past participle*.

Past Participles: ended, completed
Future Perfect Verbs in Sentences:
  This TV program *will have ended* by noon.
  By Friday, Mel *will have finished* the job.

STUDY A MODEL

Read the book jacket.

> *Present-perfect verbs are red, past-perfect verbs are blue, and future-perfect verbs are green.*

Critics have praised T. Smith, author of *Jewel Heist*, as "a sparkling voice in the mystery genre." Smith has written another gem, *The Ruby Caper*. Previously, the character Riva Barnes had solved the mystery of missing emeralds by the end of the final chapter. By the end of the first chapter of this new novel, Riva will have uncovered another mystery. She will reveal how a jewel thief had escaped before his heist was discovered. Few readers will have guessed the answer by the turn of the last page.

In the first sentence, *have praised* is in the present perfect tense, referring to something that began in the past (praising) and continues in the present.

Had solved is in the past perfect tense, referring to something that happened (solving a mystery) in the past before something else happened in the past (the end of the final chapter).

Will have guessed is in the future perfect tense, referring to something (guessing) that will be completed by a certain time in the future (by the time readers turn the last page of the book).

PRACTICE

A *Read each sentence. Label the underlined verb phrase as Present Perfect, Past Perfect, or Future Perfect.*

1. The economy <u>has prospered</u> under his administration.
2. By next week, Eileen <u>will have launched</u> her new business.
3. Frank <u>had performed</u> flawlessly before he lost his balance.
4. Cynthia's business <u>has expanded</u> over the years.
5. Before the party, Aurora <u>had made</u> delicious tacos.
6. Manuel <u>will have earned</u> enough credits by next semester.
7. <u>Has</u> Yuriko <u>left</u> the crowded banquet hall?

B *For each sentence, write the verb in the tense that is indicated.*

1. I (*find*, past perfect) my keys just before I reached the front door.
2. The power company (*restore*, future perfect) electricity by tomorrow.
3. Many civilizations (*share*, present perfect) their creation myths.
4. Roger (*hear*, present perfect) this Beethoven symphony before.
5. If we're lucky, the travel agent (*reserve*, future perfect) seats on that flight.
6. During last month's meeting, Marjie (*speak*, past perfect) to the council.
7. Kris (*study*, past perfect) for many hours prior to the history test.

C *Read the paragraph. Change the tense of the 6 underlined verbs to the present perfect, the past perfect, or the future perfect tense. Use the tense that makes sense in the context.*

This year, the drought <u>lasted</u> all summer. Some restrictions on water use <u>remained</u> due to the lack of rain. Predictions indicate that by the end of August, we <u>received</u> only three inches of rainfall, far less than the usual amount for summertime. Last summer, our average rainfall <u>reached</u> at least 10 inches by autumn. If showers fall in the next few weeks, then the water level in reservoirs <u>risen</u> to normal. During previous droughts, our community <u>suffered</u> serious weather-related problems, including forest fires and strict limits on household water consumption.

> The **present perfect, past perfect, and future perfect tenses** of verbs are formed by combining a helping verb with a past participle.

WRITE

Write the book jacket for a real or an imaginary book. Use verbs in the present, past, and future perfect tenses.

Writing Tip

Whenever possible, use **exact verbs** instead of vague, general verbs.

General	Exact
look	gape, gawk, gaze, peer, stare
plan	calculate, conspire, contrive, design, draft, plot, scheme
sleep	doze, drowse, repose, slumber, snooze

SUBJECT-VERB AGREEMENT

THINK ABOUT

Subjects and verbs must agree in number.

Use a **singular verb** with a **singular subject**.
> Melissa *enjoys* art class.
> She *paints* portraits.

Use a **plural verb** with a **plural subject**.
> The *roses* **are** yellow.
> *They* **arrange** flowers.

Use a **plural verb** with a **compound subject** joined by *and* or *both . . . and*.
> Pepper and salt **add** zest.
> Both the entree and the salad **taste** delicious.

Make sure the subject and the verb agree when the **verb comes before the subject** in a sentence.

> Out of the pond **march** the *ducks*.
> Where **is** the *captain*?
> When **is** *lunch*?

When a **compound subject** is joined by *or*, *either . . . or*, or *neither . . . nor*, the verb should agree with the closer subject.
> *Either Fran or the twins* **guide** us every year.
> *Neither your map nor this almanac* **helps**.
> *A tendon or muscles* **were** injured.

Use a **singular verb** when a subject is a **collective noun** that refers to the group as a whole.
> Our *family* **goes** on vacation in July.
> The *team* **plays** in the series each year.
> Their whole *group* **votes** in the election.
> The *flock* **rises** at a signal by its leader.

Use a **plural verb** when a subject is a **collective noun** that refers to the individual members of the group.
> All my *family* **pose** for the photograph.
> The *band* **tune** their instruments.
> The *audience* **have** good views of the stage.
> The *flock* always **return** to their home.

STUDY A MODEL

Read these notes about baking bread on a cooking show.

A crowd gathers in the kitchen. Chef Otis Farraday tries a new recipe. He and his assistants demonstrate how to make bread. Water and flour create a dough. Either Otis or his helpers knead the dough. Otis or an assistant places the bowl of dough in a warm place. As usual, neither the counters nor the sink has any space. Sitting around the set, the audience ask their questions. Suddenly Otis and his assistants are unhappy. The dough is not rising properly. They forget the yeast sometimes!

Singular subjects and verbs are red, and plural subjects and verbs are blue.

The plural verb *create* agrees with the compound subject *Water and flour*.

The singular verb *places* agrees with the closer subject, *assistant*.

The singular verb *has* agrees with the closer subject, *sink*.

The plural verb *ask* agrees with the collective noun *audience*, which refers to the audience as individual members.

PRACTICE

A *For each sentence, write the letter of the verb that completes the sentence and agrees with the subject.*

1. The company __C__ computer parts.
2. Both the students and the teacher __B__ at the joke.
3. These trucks __A__ fresh produce.
4. Neither the ice cream shop nor the deli __E__ early.
5. Our team __D__ each another during the game.
6. He __F__ any knowledge of the prank.
7. The sauce or the chili peppers __G__ spicy.

A transport
B laugh
C produces
D cheer
E opens
F denies
G taste

B *Read each sentence. Write the verb in parentheses that agrees with the subject.*

1. The teacher (criticizes, criticize) her students' performance.
2. Several freighters (has docked, have docked) in the harbor.
3. Either beans or corn (grows, grow) well in this climate.
4. Both wind and rain (causes, cause) soil erosion.
5. The United States (border, borders) Canada.
6. Olivia and I (eat, eats) the pudding.
7. Our group (works, work) well with each other.
8. Where (is, are) your cousin?

C *Read the paragraph. Rewrite it, correcting the 7 errors in subject-verb agreement. Use underlining for italics.*

> *Starry Night* is a famous painting by Vincent Van Gogh. Our entire class have seen this painting in the Museum of Modern Art. The brush strokes and color is strong and bold. Bright stars whirls across the canvas. Both round hills and a small village dots the landscape. Neither the houses nor the single church look inhabited. The church spire and tall cypress trees is pointing straight into the sky. Our class ask their questions about the painting. The museum guide or our teachers tells about Van Gogh's masterpiece.

A verb must agree with its subject in number.

WRITE

Write a recipe for a favorite family dish. Ask an adult for details if necessary. Name all the ingredients, tell how to prepare the dish, and tell how long to cook or chill it. Write in the present tense, and make sure that subjects and verbs agree.

Writing Tip

A **compound subject** can consist of more than two items.

Melanie and Leo often walk in the park.

Melanie's mother, father, aunt, and uncle sometimes come along.

Neither snow nor rain nor heat nor gloom of night stays these couriers from the swift completion of their appointed rounds. (postal service motto)

THINK ABOUT

Subjects and **verbs** must agree in number. Sometimes a subject is an indefinite pronoun. An **indefinite pronoun** refers to *a person, place, or thing that is not specific.*

Singular Indefinite Pronouns: *another, anybody, anyone, anything, each, either, everybody, everyone, everything, much, neither, nobody, no one, nothing, one, other, somebody, someone, something*

Use a **singular verb** when the **subject** of a sentence is a **singular indefinite pronoun.**

> *Each **plays** the game.*   *No one **loses.***
> *Is somebody lost?*   *Nothing **explains** it.*

Plural Indefinite Pronouns: *both, few, many, ones, others, several*

Use a **plural verb** when the **subject** of a sentence is a **plural indefinite pronoun.**

> *Few **understand** the rules.*   *Many **have** pets.*
> *Several **are** broken.*   *Both **win** a prize.*

Singular or Plural Indefinite Pronouns: *all, any, more, most, none, some*

Use **either a singular or a plural verb** with *all, any, more, most, none,* or *some* as a subject depending on the object of the preposition that follows the subject.

> *Most <u>of the merchandise</u> **is** on sale.*
> *Most <u>of the items</u> **are** on sale.*
> *All <u>of the pie</u> **is** gone.*
> *All <u>of the cookies</u> **are** gone.*

However, don't be confused by **phrases** that come between other subjects and verbs in sentences.

> The *information* in the reports ***was*** alarming.
> Two *reporters* on the news show ***give*** scores.
> My *cousin*, one of the cheerleaders, ***leads*** the first cheer.
> The *cheerleaders*, part of the pep squad, ***have*** spirit.

STUDY A MODEL

Read this message found inside an old bottle.

Nobody knows what misfortune has befallen me and my crewmates. Our ship, Pretty Maiden, was wrecked on September 21, 1788. A fierce storm with huge waves and high winds was our undoing. Sadly, our fine vessel sank. Now most of my shipmates are starving. Several are seriously injured. Unfortunately, none of the sailors have a map, compass, or sextant to fix our location on this deserted island. If anyone finds this message, please send help.

Singular subjects and verbs are red. Plural subjects and verbs are blue.

The indefinite pronoun *Nobody* is singular and agrees with the singular verb *knows*.

In the third sentence, the singular subject *storm* agrees with the singular verb *was*, even though the plural word *winds* comes directly in front of the verb.

Most is a plural subject and agrees with the plural verb *are starving* because *shipmates*, the object of the preposition *of*, is plural. *Several* is a plural subject and agrees with *are*. Here, *none* is a plural subject and agrees with the verb *have*.

Anyone is a singular subject and agrees with the singular verb *finds*.

PRACTICE

A *Read each sentence. Write the verb that agrees with the underlined subject.*

1. <u>None</u> of the pizzas (is, are) left.
2. (Was, Were) <u>everything</u> destroyed by the blaze?
3. <u>Others</u> (believes, believe) quite differently.
4. <u>Something</u> (smells, smell) rotten.
5. A <u>tunnel</u> through the mountains (is, are) open.
6. <u>Some</u> of the assignments (is, are) difficult.
7. Front-row <u>seats</u>, the best vantage point, (fills, fill) quickly.

B *Read each sentence. Write the subject and the verb that agrees with it.*

1. Ships in the harbor (lies, lie) at anchor.
2. None of the armor (requires, require) polishing.
3. Nothing (is, are) accomplished after a long meeting.
4. The volunteers, members of a local church, (cleans, clean) the park.
5. (Was, Were) the director of special events present?
6. Someone (challenges, challenge) the referee's ruling.
7. (Does, Do) both match the new wallpaper?
8. Many of the members (has, have) called.

C *Read the paragraph. Rewrite it, correcting the 10 errors in subject-verb agreement.*

Hiking, one of the most enjoyable forms of exercise, require little equipment or training. When preparing for a hike, most of the more experienced hikers packs first-aid kits. Others fills knapsacks with extra food, water, and clothing. Everyone wear a watch, and somebody usually bring a compass. One of the most important rules are quite clear. Everyone must stay on the marked trail. Few follows short cuts because they might get lost. An unmarked trail in the woods pose danger. Potentially, lost hikers without a sense of direction becomes disoriented, dehydrated, or exhausted. Fortunately, trail maps, an essential item, leads the way back to civilization.

An indefinite pronoun subject and **a subject followed by a phrase** must agree with verbs in number.

WRITE

Imagine that you are lost on a deserted island. Write a message that you might send in a bottle. Use the present tense and make sure that singular and plural subjects and verbs agree.

Writing Tip

A **negative word** is a word that means "no" or "not." When you write, avoid using double negatives, which often mean the opposite of what you want to say.

Double Negative: Milo did not find no gold in the old sea chest.

Intended Meaning: Milo did not find gold in the old sea chest.

Actual Meaning: Milo found gold in the old sea chest.

ADJECTIVES

THINK ABOUT

What color is your shirt? How many friends sit at your table during lunch? **Adjectives** supply this kind of information and can make your writing more specific, informative, and colorful.

An **adjective** describes a noun or pronoun by telling *what kind, how many, how much,* or *which one.*

What Kind: Whales are **mammoth** *mammals.*
How Many: *Three whales* breached.
How Much: *Most spectators* gasped.
Which One(s): Wipe *these* chairs with *that* cloth.
We will take the *next* bus.

- Adjectives can come *before* or *after* the noun or pronoun they describe.
Before: The *weary runners* took a rest.
After: The *runners,* **weary,** took a rest.
The *runners* were **weary,** and they took a rest.

- Most adjectives have a **positive,** a **comparative,** and a **superlative** degree.
Use the **positive degree** when no comparison is being made.

This *album* is **new.**

Here is a *popular CD.*

Use the **comparative degree** when comparing two nouns or pronouns. To form the comparative degree, add *er* to most short adjectives or add the word *more* to most long adjectives.

This *album* is **newer** than that one. (*new + er*)

This *CD* is **more popular** than that *CD.* (*popular + more*)

Use the **superlative degree** when comparing three or more nouns or pronouns. To form the superlative degree, add *est* to most short adjectives or add the word *most* to most long adjectives.

This *album* is the **newest** in the shop. (*new + est*)

Here is the **most popular** *CD* ever recorded by Flash in the Pan. (*popular + most*)

Avoid double comparisons. Do not use *more* or *most* with adjectives that end in *er* or *est.*

Incorrect: This color is *more lighter* than that one.
This is the *most heaviest* of all the boxes.

Correct: This color is *lighter.*
This is the *heaviest* box of all.

- Some adjectives have special comparative and superlative forms: *good, better, best; bad, worse, worst; many, more, most.*
- Some adjectives, such as *unique* or *circular,* cannot have comparative or superlative degrees.

STUDY A MODEL

Read this paragraph about yo-yos.

The yo-yo is ancient. This toy probably got its name from a word meaning "to return." Hunters in the Philippines used wood disks as weapons. They dropped the disks from trees and then hauled up the heavy disks with twine and dropped them again. In the 1920s, Pedro Flores brought the first yo-yo from the Philippines to the United States. Today, many people around the world play with yo-yos. Some players can make yo-yos "sleep," and others do harder tricks. But those players who compete in national contests are the most skilled.

Adjectives telling what kind *are red, those telling* how many *or* how much *are blue, and those telling* which one(s) *are green.*

- *Ancient* comes after *yo-yo* and tells *what kind* of yo-yo.

- *Wood* and *heavy* tell *what kind* of disks.

- *First* tells *which* yo-yo.

- *Many* tells *how many* people.

- *Harder* is in the comparative degree.

- *Most skilled* is in the superlative degree and tells *what kind* of players.

PRACTICE

A *Write each adjective under the correct heading.*

1. enormous 3. seven 5. several 7. first
2. these 4. graceful 6. next 8. grumpy

What Kind	How Many or How Much	Which One(s)

B *Read each sentence. Write the comparative or superlative degree of the adjective in parentheses.*

1. Football is a (rough) sport than baseball.
2. Which is (swift), a cheetah or a cougar?
3. This is the (magnificent) room in the palace.
4. Be careful; that is the (deep) part of the pool!
5. Kei is the (mechanical) student in shop class.
6. China is the (populous) country in the world.
7. The Blue Fountain has (delicious) food than The Milano has.

C *Read the paragraph. Write the 23 adjectives that modify the underlined nouns or pronouns. Do not include articles. Correct any double comparisons by drawing a line through* **more** *or* **most**.

Rising from the Adriatic, Corfu is an island of brilliant <u>light</u> and lush <u>countryside</u>. Lying between the two <u>countries</u> of Albania and Italy, Corfu beckons in the balmy <u>sea</u>. This small <u>island</u> is diverse. Since its northeastern <u>end</u> is more sheltered, those <u>settings</u> for snorkeling, fishing, and swimming range from rough <u>surf</u> to more calmer <u>lagoons</u>. Most <u>tourists</u> enjoy several <u>beaches</u>. The island is a mountainous <u>one</u>, boasting fertile <u>valleys</u> and numerous <u>lakes</u>. Many olive <u>trees</u> from ancient <u>times</u> abound, and some <u>wildflowers</u> of the most brightest <u>hues</u> bloom abundantly. <u>Corfu</u> is most unique!

An **adjective** describes a noun or pronoun by telling *what kind, how many* or *how much,* or *which one(s)*.

WRITE

Write a paragraph describing the history or background of a person, place, or thing that you are familiar with. Use vivid adjectives and correct comparative and superlative forms to paint a realistic picture for readers.

Writing Tip

When you write, keep in mind that a word can be used as **more than one part of speech**, depending on how you use it in a sentence.

Where's the *dog*? (noun)
Where's the *dog* blanket? (adjective)
Were you in the *play*? (noun)
Which part did you *play*? (verb)
Let's read the *play* reviews. (adjective)
Please give me *some*. (pronoun)
I would like *some* cider. (adjective)

23

ADVERBS

THINK ABOUT

Do you finish your homework *quickly* or *slowly*? Do you *frequently* arrive early for class? **Adverbs** provide this kind of information and can make your writing more informative and descriptive.

An **adverb** describes a verb by telling *how*, *when*, or *where*. An adverb also describes an adjective or another adverb by telling *how much* or *to what extent*. An adverb often, but not always, ends in *ly*.

How: Bluejays *chattered* **noisily**.

When: Birds **often** *eat* seeds and berries.

Where: We *hung* the birdfeeder **outside**.

How Much: The chickadees are **extremely** *hungry*.

To What Extent: Hawks fly **very** *fast*.

- An adverb can come at the beginning or at the end of a sentence.
  Suddenly Sue laughed. Sue laughed **suddenly**.
- Use a comma after an introductory adverb if you want readers to pause.
  Fortunately, we won.

- An adverb can come *before* or *after* the verb.
  Lia **quickly** changed. Lia changed **quickly**.
- An adverb can come between the helping verb and the main verb in a verb phrase.
  Firefighters *have* **usually** *arrived* quickly.
- Most adverbs have a **positive**, a **comparative**, and a **superlative** degree.

Use the **positive degree** when no comparison is being made.
  Will this meteor shower begin *soon*?

Use the **comparative degree** to compare two actions. To form the comparative degree, add *er* to most short adverbs or add the word *more* to most long adverbs.
  Tim ran *faster* than ever before. (*fast + er*)
  Ted eats *more slowly* than I do. (*more + slowly*)

Use the **superlative degree** to compare three or more actions. To form the superlative degree, add *est* to most short adverbs or add the word *most* to most long adverbs.
  The third wave broke the *hardest*. (*hard + est*)
  Of all subjects, I study science *most carefully*. (*most + carefully*)

Avoid double comparisons. Do not use *more* or *most* with adverbs that end in *er* or *est*.
  Incorrect: I run *more faster*. **Correct:** I run *faster*.

STUDY A MODEL

Read this set of directions.

Directions

First, open the box. Then examine the contents thoroughly. Pieces are quite rarely omitted, but mistakes do happen sometimes. Next, read the rather easy instructions. Make sure you understand all of the very important steps and diagrams. Arrange the really large parts near your workspace. You will assemble this truly classic bench more easily than any other home project that you have done.

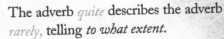

Adverbs that tell how, when, *or* where *are red; adverbs that tell* how much *or* to what extent *are blue.*

 The adverb *First* tells *when*.

 The adverb *quite* describes the adverb *rarely*, telling *to what extent*.

 The adverb *rather* describes the adjective *easy*, telling *to what extent*.

 Very tells *to what extent* about the adjective *important*.

Near tells *where* about the verb *arrange*.

 More easily is in the comparative degree.

PRACTICE

A *Read each phrase. Write the underlined adverb under the correct heading.*

1. <u>gently</u> washing
2. swam <u>yesterday</u>
3. flying <u>everywhere</u>
4. <u>eagerly</u> awaiting
5. <u>never</u> saw
6. <u>nearly</u> perfect
7. ran <u>around</u>
8. <u>slightly</u> round

How	When	Where	To What Extent or How Much

B *Read each sentence. Write the comparative or superlative degree of the adverb in parentheses.*

1. The first hot-air balloon soared (high) than the second one.
2. Fix this lamp so that it shines (brightly) than that one.
3. Of all the volunteers, Mayuko has worked (quickly).
4. The guides arrived (late) than the tourists did!
5. Which of the three babysitters behaves (responsibly)?
6. The last row of the chorus should sing the (loud).
7. The upper trail slopes (steeply) than the lower trail.

C *Read the paragraph. Write the positive, comparative, or superlative degree of each of the 10 adverbs in parentheses.*

Clive arrives (early) at his new job than he did at his old job. He (happily) sells pennants and programs at the baseball stadium. Of all the vendors, he works (efficiently) and (confidently), and he sells his items very (quickly). Clive chose this job (thoughtfully) than the one he had last summer. Of all the jobs that Clive has had, this one (clearly) fulfills him. His supervisor treats him (fairly) than did his previous boss. After work, Clive (proudly) tells his family about the day's sales and the highlights of the game. His play-by-play accounts are given (skillfully) than those given by the local TV sports announcer.

An **adverb** describes a verb by telling *how, when,* or *where.* It also describes an adjective or another adverb by telling *to what* extent or *how much.*

WRITE

Write about an outdoor activity that you enjoy, such as rollerblading, shooting hoops, or cross-country skiing. Use precise adverbs and appropriate comparative or superlative degrees to describe the actions involved in this activity.

Writing Tip

Below are some adverbs that are sometimes called **intensifiers**. They modify adjectives or other adverbs (never verbs) by telling *how much* or *to what extent.*

almost	least	rather	terribly
enormously	less	really	thoroughly
extremely	more	so	truly
fully	most	slightly	totally
hardly	nearly	sometimes	too
just	quite	somewhat	very

ADJECTIVES AND ADVERBS

THINK ABOUT

Adjectives and adverbs are both modifiers. When you write, be careful not to confuse an adjective with an adverb.

- **Adjectives** modify, or describe, *nouns* or *pronouns*.

  The *perilous road* was closed.
  Accurate answers are required on a test.
  She was **rude** to the sales clerk.

- **Adverbs** modify *verbs, adjectives,* or other *adverbs*.

  "No way," she **rudely** *replied*.
  The road is **perilously** *steep*.
  Trina answered the questions **very** *carefully*.

  - Adjectives and adverbs are sometimes confused when they follow *verbs*.
    Adjectives often follow **linking verbs** such as *is, are, was, become, seem, appear, look, sound, smell, taste,* or *feel*.
      Sam *feels* **nervous**. The child *is* **angry**.
    Adverbs often follow **action verbs**.
      Sam *fidgets* **nervously**. The child *yells* **angrily**.

- The words *bad, good, real,* and *sure* are **adjectives**.
    One skier had a **bad** *fall*.
    Is Boyd a **good** *artist*?
    The restaurant has a **real** *goldfish pond*.
    Lily is **sure** about her decision.

- The words *badly, really,* and *surely* are **adverbs**.
    His leg is **badly** *broken*.
    The restaurant is **really** *busy*.
    That driver is **surely** *brave*!

- The word *well* is usually an **adverb**. When it describes a state of health, however, it is an **adjective**.
    Adverbs
    The class *behaved* **well** during the assembly.
    Police dogs are **well** *trained*.
    Adjectives
    Obviously, the panda does not *feel* **well**.
    Will Kim *be* **well** before the Snow Ball?

STUDY A MODEL

Read this food critic's column.

VegHaven recently opened on Main Street. The menu offers real variety, from lentil burgers to tofu desserts. Daily specials are very well prepared. Because this is an extremely popular spot, more seats are badly needed. Still, the service is always efficient, and the food is consistently good. The dim lights should be replaced, but otherwise the restaurant is quite cozy. Diners clearly enjoy the soft music in the background. VegHaven is always busy, so arrive early.

The red words are adjectives.
The blue words are adverbs.

In the first sentence, *recently* is an adverb modifying the verb *opened*.

The adverb *very* modifies another adverb, *well*, which modifies the verb *are prepared*.

Consistently is an adverb modifying the adjective *good*, which modifies the noun *food*.

Quite modifies *cozy*, which modifies the noun *restaurant*.

Always is an adverb modifying the adjective *busy*, and *early* modifies the verb *arrive*.

PRACTICE

A *Read the sentences. Label each of the 14 underlined words Adjective or Adverb.*

1. An <u>unfortunate</u> accident <u>really</u> tied up traffic.
2. <u>Several</u> volunteers were stranded <u>accidentally</u>.
3. <u>Huge</u> floodlights shone <u>brightly</u> in the stadium.
4. "Is he <u>very</u> <u>reliable</u>?" asked my neighbor.
5. Cara looked <u>intently</u> at the tank of <u>tropical</u> fish.
6. After the fire, <u>polluted</u> air drifted <u>slowly</u> over the city.
7. Toby has a <u>surprisingly</u> <u>good</u> idea for the benefit.

B *Read each sentence. Write the adjective or adverb that correctly completes it.*

1. Jason trudged home (slow, slowly).
2. The science fair featured (real, really) interesting projects.
3. Inspector Brown glanced at the (suspicious, suspiciously) box.
4. Walk (quick, quickly) to the nearest exit.
5. The cheerleaders performed their routine (good, well).
6. The feverish child has a (bad, badly) cold.
7. James seems (sure, surely) that he is right.

C *Read the paragraph. Write the 12 words that correctly complete it.*

During the time of Queen Elizabeth I, a vein of (real, really) (pure, purely) graphite was discovered in the Borrowdale Valley of northern England. The graphite left an (obvious, obviously) streak when it was rubbed against a (smooth, smoothly) surface. This (accidental, accidentally) discovery lead to the creation of a (popular, popularly) writing instrument, the pencil. The soft English graphite could be cut (even, evenly) into rods, but it crumpled (easy, easily). Users ended up with (bad, badly) dirtied hands. A (good, well) solution to this problem was the invention of metal or wood holders. These holders were (usual, usually) (fair, fairly) expensive.

Adjectives and **adverbs** are modifiers. Adjectives modify *nouns* or *pronouns*. Adverbs modify *verbs*, *adjectives*, or other *adverbs*.

WRITE

Write a paragraph for a news column. Tell about a favorite business (a shop, a restaurant, a supermarket) in your community. Use descriptive adjectives and adverbs correctly.

Writing Tip

A **prepositional phrase** can act as an **adjective**.

The pack *on the shelf* is yours.
   (tells which one)

Kittens *with stripes* are rare.
   (tells what kind)

A **prepositional phrase** can act as an **adverb**.

My cup fell *off the table*. (tells where)

Meet Roberto and me *at noon*. (tells when)

27

HOMOPHONES

THINK ABOUT

Homophones are words that sound alike but have different meanings and spellings. Here are a few examples:

bare, bear — Can that brown *bear bear* to climb up the *bare* winter tree?

cent, scent, sent — I hope Aunt Bea didn't spend a *cent* on the foul-smelling *scent* that she *sent* for my birthday.

bridal, bridle — The *bridal* party posed while the carriage driver held the horse's *bridle*.

buy, by — Would you *buy* a quart of milk if you stop *by* the store?

capital, capitol — Visit the historic *capitol* building in our state's *capital*.

do, due — They *do* homework carefully if a difficult assignment is *due*.

guessed, guest — Holmes *guessed* that the one-eyed man was a hotel *guest*.

pause, paws — My cat will *pause* briefly while she licks her white *paws*.

read, red — Fred easily *read* the big white letters on that *red* stop sign.

road, rode — The bicyclists *rode* on the dusty, bumpy *road*.

weak, week — I felt *weak* from the flu for a *week*.

Some homophones include a **contraction.**

it's, its — *It's* clear that the truck lost *its* brakes before the accident.

their, there, they're — *They're* going *there* when they finish *their* chores.

you're, your — Congratulations! *You're* the winner of *your* school's writing contest.

who's, whose — *Who's* the unlucky person *whose* gloves were lost?

STUDY A MODEL

Read this nature poem written in couplets.

Questions

A question asked by a grizzly bear:
Whose scent do I smell in the air?
A question asked by a mouse in snow:
Do tracks of my paws show there I go?
A question asked by a red fox on a road:
Can I outrun trucks carrying their load?
A question asked by loudly honking geese:
What message is sent in half-bare trees?
A question asked by a bumpy green frog:
Which fly has guessed I'm on this log?
A question asked by a rabbit in a meadow:
Who's the guest in your garden now?

The homophones are red.

◄ The word *bear* in the first couplet, or pair of rhyming lines, is a noun, while *bare* in the fourth couplet is an adjective.

◄ In the first couplet, *scent* is a noun, while *sent* in the fourth couplet is a verb.

◄ In the second couplet, *there* is an adverb, while *their* in the third couplet is a possessive pronoun.

◄ In the fifth couplet, *guessed* is a verb, while *guest* in the sixth couplet is a noun.

PRACTICE

A *Read the sentences. Write the 9 words that correctly complete them.*

1. The (capital, capitol) was renovated last winter.
2. Is (your, you're) report about the book you recently (red, read)?
3. Go left at the fork in the (rode, road) to get (their, they're, there).
4. Alicia is the girl (who's, whose) job application is (do, due) today.
5. Scientists found the (bare, bear) by following (its, it's) tracks.

B *Read each sentence. Rewrite the incorrect homophone. If there is no incorrect homophone, write Correct.*

1. The capital of Minnesota is St. Paul.
2. Hit the paws button to stop the video.
3. Have you correctly guest the number of jellybeans in the jar?
4. Who's the candidate speaking at tonight's rally?
5. "Your going to be terribly late!" Barbara said.

C *Read the paragraphs. Rewrite the paragraphs, including the words that correctly complete them.*

Trish and Janette (red, read) the wedding invitation that (their, they're, there) cousin Meeya had (cent, scent, sent). The ceremony was planned for June.

"Let's shop for a (bridal, bridle) present tomorrow," said Janette.

"(Your, You're) right! We (do, due) not have too much time," said Trish.

The two friends got a ride to the mall. (Their, They're, There) they tried to (buy, by) a suitable gift. (Buy, By) noon they felt exhausted.

"(Its, It's) hard to find the perfect present," sighed Janette.

Finally, Trish and Janette decided to purchase (guessed, guest) passes to a health spa. They (guessed, guest) that a special day of relaxation would be appreciated by the engaged couple (who's, whose) schedule was hectic.

"Done!" exclaimed Janette. "Now we're (do, due) some lunch before we go home."

Homophones are words that sound alike but have different meanings and spellings.

WRITE

Write a silly or serious poem or a short story in which you use a few pairs of homophones correctly. Circle each homophone.

Writing Tip

The following **words**, though not homophones, are often **confused**. Be careful to write these words correctly.

desert (a place)   later (time)
dessert (food)   latter (the second thing)

lay (to place)   real (adjective)
lie (to recline)   really, very (adverbs)

SIMPLE, COMPOUND, AND COMPLEX SENTENCES

LESSON 14

THINK ABOUT

When you write, use different kinds of sentences: **simple**, **compound**, and **complex**.

- A **simple sentence** contains one *independent clause*. A **clause** is a group of words that has both a subject and a predicate. An **independent clause** expresses a complete thought and can stand alone.

      s   p   s   p

    The old king agrees.   The blue vase broke.

A simple sentence, which is one independent clause, can have a *compound subject* or a *compound predicate*.

    s   p

    She *sketches and paints* in oils.

    s   p

    The dog and the bird are friends.

- A **compound sentence** contains two or more *independent clauses* that are either joined together by a **comma** and a **coordinating conjunction** *(and, or, but, nor, for,* or *yet)* or by a semicolon.
  Compound sentences:
      The doorbell rang, *and* Larry walked in.
      A siren blared, *but* the baby did not wake up.
      My report is due Tuesday; my first draft is done.
      Shelves were stocked; sale items were displayed.

- A **complex sentence** contains one **independent clause** and one or more **dependent clauses**.
  A **dependent clause** is a group of words that has a subject and a predicate but cannot stand alone because it does not express a complete thought. It requires an independent clause to complete its meaning. A dependent clause begins with a **relative pronoun** *(who, whom, whose, which,* or *that)* or with a **subordinating conjunction** such as *after, although, as, because, before, if, since, unless, until, when,* or *while.* Use a **comma** after a dependent clause that begins a sentence.
      When my cat sleeps, she snores.
  The dependent clause *when my cat sleeps* doesn't make sense and can't stand alone. It needs the independent clause *she snores* to tell what happens.
  Complex sentences:
      Jo bought a house *that was built in 1930.*
      Although yesterday was rainy, today is sunny.
        Remember to use commas to set off a
        dependent clause that is *not essential*
        to the sentence.
      Mrs. Dow, *who teaches English,* will retire soon.

STUDY A MODEL

Read this biographical sketch of Nellie Bly.

Elizabeth Cochran was born in Pennsylvania on May 5, 1864. She trained to be a teacher, but she later became one of the first women in investigative journalism. In 1885, the Pittsburgh Dispatch hired her after she wrote an eloquent letter to the newspaper. Cochran began to publish her stories, and she took the pen name Nellie Bly. As a journalist, Bly focused on social problems. The adventurous Bly also made a record-breaking trip around the world, which was sponsored by a newspaper. After a full career, Bly died in 1922.

Simple sentences are red, compound sentences are blue, and complex sentences are green.

◀ This simple sentence has one independent clause. The subject is *Elizabeth Cochran,* and the predicate is *was born in Pennsylvania on May 5, 1864.*

◀ This complex sentence contains one independent clause, *In 1885, the Pittsburgh Dispatch hired her,* and one dependent clause, *after she wrote an eloquent letter to the newspaper.*

◀ The next-to-last sentence is complex. It ends in a dependent clause that is not essential to the meaning of the sentence and is therefore set off with a comma.

30

PRACTICE

A *Read each clause. Label the clause **D** for dependent or **I** for independent.*

1. the wild horses fled
2. while the barn burned
3. the store was crowded
4. although the sale was over
5. whom the students elected
6. the man and his son laughed
7. who marched in the parade
8. several band members also sing

B *Read the sentences. Write the 10 independent clauses and the 3 dependent clauses.*

1. Because I overslept, I missed the bus.
2. The crowd cheered the team enthusiastically.
3. Milana goes to ballet class, and Vienna takes gymnastics.
4. Barbara read the map, but she could not find Elm Street.
5. You'll save time if you take the express train.
6. The kitchen faucet leaks; Kay will hire a plumber.
7. The owner whose horse won the race entered the winner's circle.

C *Read the paragraph. Label each of the 13 sentences **Simple**, **Compound**, or **Complex**.*

As soon as I walked into the cafeteria, I smelled the beef stew. I have always loved beef stew, and I immediately chose it for my lunch. I stood in a line that stretched forever. It was worth it, though. When it was finally my turn, the server ladled me a huge, steaming bowl of chunky beef stew. I was headed in the direction of the nearest table, but I saw my friend Hank over in the corner. I headed for him instead. Hank is also a stew-lover, and his bowl was already half gone. Mine was gone shortly too. We decided that pudding would be an excellent dessert choice. Hank and I stood in the long line together and finally got our two bowls of chocolate pudding. Before we had finished the last spoonful, lunch was over. Hank and I ate the last bites, made after-school plans, and then headed back to class.

A **simple sentence** contains one independent clause. A **compound sentence** contains two or more independent clauses joined together by a comma and a coordinating conjunction or by a semicolon. A **complex sentence** contains one independent clause and one or more dependent clauses.

WRITE

Write a biographical sketch of a person you know or have read about. Include simple, compound, and complex sentences.

Writing Tip

Here are some more **subordinating conjunctions**.

as far as	even though
as if	once
as long as	so that
as soon as	though
as though	whenever
even if	wherever

THINK ABOUT

Words, phrases, and clauses that give information about, or modify, other words are called **modifiers**.

To avoid confusion, place *modifiers* as close as possible to the words that they describe.

Unclear: The bird perched on a twig, a cardinal.

Clear: The bird, *a cardinal*, perched on a twig.

Unclear: Writing a prescription, the dog barked at the veterinarian.

Clear: The dog barked at the veterinarian *writing a prescription*.

Unclear: A farmer is selling a donkey in overalls.

Clear: A farmer *in overalls* is selling a donkey.

Unclear: Recently finished, shoppers crowd the mall.

Clear: Shoppers crowd the *recently finished* mall.

Unclear: Cars of the late 1950s are the favorites of my uncles with their huge fins.

Clear: Cars of the late 1950s, *with their huge fins*, are favorites of my uncles.

Unclear: With a fluffy tail, Tim laughed at the spritely gray squirrel.

Clear: Tim laughed at the spritely gray squirrel *with a fluffy tail*.

Unclear: The reunion that overlooks the river took place at a restaurant.

Clear: The reunion took place at a restaurant *that overlooks the river*.

The meaning of a sentence can change depending on the placement of a modifier.

Julie *only* goes to the library at night.
Julie goes *only* to the library at night.
Only Julie goes to the library at night.

STUDY A MODEL

Read this CD review.

Don't miss the recording by Out of Touch. These West Coast musicians, with their experimental sound, have fans around the country. Every Dog Must Have His Day, the band's first CD, sold millions of copies and earned them richly deserved acclaim. Their latest effort, which has a slightly Latin flavor, showcases the group's daring. Weaving together different musical traditions, Out of Touch takes a risk. When the lead singer performs, he will move every listener who hears him.

The modifiers, which are placed correctly, are red.

Notice that the phrase *with their experimental sound* is placed next to *musicians*, the word it modifies.

The phrase *the band's first CD* follows *Every Dog Must Have His Day*, the words that it modifies.

The clause *which has a slightly Latin flavor* follows *effort*, which it modifies.

When the lead singer performs modifies *will move*, telling *when*.

The clause *who hears him* is correctly placed after *listener*, which it modifies.

PRACTICE

A *Read each sentence. Rewrite it, correcting the misplaced modifier. If there are no misplaced modifiers, write* **Correct.**

1. The monkey ate the banana with orange fur.
2. The class listened to the guest speaker, sitting quietly.
3. Rarely cleaned, Frieda scowled at the oven.
4. Susan's car, a hybrid, uses less gasoline.
5. The author signed a copy of her book, who had won a prize.
6. Josh walked his dog Pete who was late for work.
7. Excited and pleased, Rita accepted the gift.
8. One reporter criticized the speech who covers politics.

B *Read the sentences. Rewrite them, correcting the misplaced modifiers.*

1. The baby smiled at the man in the stroller.
2. Andy works for the company's president, a secretary.
3. The van stopped at the light carrying crates of apples.
4. This documentary won an award, which examines civil rights.
5. Bright and crackling, the campers were warmed by the fire.
6. Tightly stacked, the workers used a crane to move the steel beams.
7. Your jacket is beside my cap with a hood.
8. The baby smiled at his mother in the blue snowsuit.

C *Read the paragraph. Rewrite it, correcting the 5 misplaced modifiers.*

Our piano needed tuning, which is 50 years old. Mr. Fielding, the piano tuner, politely introduced himself to my mother, carrying a black case. Patiently and slowly, he removed a tuning fork that was out of tune to identify each note. He used a special tool to tune the pins that looked like a socket wrench. After Mr. Fielding had worked for two hours, he finally finished. Then my mother thanked Mr. Fielding, who was the best pianist in the family.

To avoid confusion, place **modifiers** as close as possible to the words they describe.

WRITE

Write a brief review of a book, play, CD, or movie. Use modifiers correctly and effectively.

Writing Tip

When a modifier does not clearly modify any word in a sentence, add the needed words.

Unclear: Lost and frightened, trail markers were tacked on trees.

Clear: Lost and frightened, we looked for trail markers tacked on trees.

Unclear: After studying, the test was easily finished.

Clear: After studying, Matt easily finished the test.

SENTENCE FRAGMENTS

THINK ABOUT

The word *fragment* means "something incomplete." A **sentence fragment** is a group of words that does not express a complete thought and cannot stand alone as a sentence.

A sentence fragment may be missing a *subject*, a *predicate*, or both. Correct this type of sentence fragment by adding the missing part.
- **Fragment:** Awakened at dawn. (no subject)
  Sentence: *The campers* awakened at dawn.
- **Fragment:** A thousand miniature lights. (no predicate)
  Sentence: A thousand miniature lights *sparkled*.
- **Fragment:** Somewhere on the highway. (no subject or predicate)
  Sentence: *I should stop* somewhere on the highway.

Even though a *dependent clause* has a subject and a predicate, it still is a fragment when it stands alone because it does not state a complete thought.

> **Dependent Clause:** If the sky is clear.
> **Sentence:** *That star is visible* if the sky is clear.
> **Dependent Clause:** Who played the piano.
> **Sentence:** *I know the man* who played the piano.

A **phrase** is a group of words that does not have a subject and a predicate and does not express a complete thought. A phrase that stands alone, therefore, is a sentence fragment. To correct this kind of fragment, join it to an independent clause.

- **Phrase:** At the bottom of the pond.
  Sentences: *Trout swim* at the bottom of the pond. At the bottom of the pond, *a rock sparkled*.

- **Phrase:** Boiled in a pot.
  Sentences: Boiled in a pot, *berries become jam*. *Berries* boiled in a pot *make a tasty jam*.

- **Phrase:** The top athlete.
  Sentences: The top athlete *waved to the fans*. *We congratulated Carmen*, who is the top athlete.

- **Phrase:** Practicing overtime.
  Sentences: Practicing overtime *led to victory for our team*. Practicing overtime, *she perfected her shot*.

- **Phrase:** To volunteer at a library.
  Sentences: *Cerisse is happy* to volunteer at a library. To volunteer at a library *is a joy*.

STUDY A MODEL

Read the notes and then the published minutes for a town meeting.

Notes: The town board met. To discuss the creation of a waterfront park. A boat launch was proposed. If the town buys the land. Don Moss presented a study. A local engineer. Two board members also spoke. Who oppose the plan.

Published Minutes: The town board met to discuss the creation of a waterfront park. A boat launch was proposed if the town buys the land. Don Moss, who is a local engineer, presented a study. Two board members who oppose the plan also spoke.

Sentence fragments are red.

◄ The jotted notes are choppy and hard to read because of the many sentence fragments (*To discuss the creation of a waterfront park* and *A local engineer*, for example).

◄ Various dependent clauses have been joined to independent clauses (*Don Moss, who is a local engineer, presented a study*, for example) to create complete sentences, making the published minutes easy to read.

34

PRACTICE

A *Read each item. Label it **S** for sentence or **F** for fragment.*

1. When the smoke alarm sounded suddenly.
2. The flag fluttered.
3. Over the river and through the woods.
4. Whose giant turnip won a blue ribbon.
5. Joined the girls' field hockey team.
6. Jonathan is a storyteller who entertains children.
7. Learning the difficult rules of the game.

B *Read each item. Correct the fragment by joining it with the sentence. Add punctuation and joining words as needed.*

1. Let's buy popcorn. Before the movie begins.
2. The cashier quickly rang up the order. And put the items in a bag.
3. Maureen helped the children. In the arts and crafts class.
4. In the calm waters of the harbor. A sailboat drifted lazily.
5. A truck struggled up the hill. That pulled a heavy load.
6. Frightened by the explosion. The bystanders scattered.
7. Mr. Chung waited patiently. To enter the auditorium.

C *Read the paragraph. Rewrite it, correcting the 13 sentence fragments.*

Jeannette Rankin was born in Montana in 1880. In a small pioneer town. After she attended college. She became a social worker. Moved to Spokane, Washington, for her first job. There she met women. Who wanted the right to vote. Rankin handed out leaflets and spoke at rallies. To sway public opinion. Finally, women in Washington. Won voting rights. Then, in 1916 Rankin ran for Congress. The first woman elected to the House of Representatives. Where she worked for peace. In 1917, she courageously voted against involvement in World War I. Defeated in a bid for the Senate in 1918. Rankin successfully ran again for Congress in 1940. Fighting for peace. Was again Rankin's focus.

A **sentence fragment** is a group of words that does not express a complete thought and cannot stand alone as a sentence.

WRITE

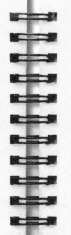

Write minutes for an imaginary school meeting, in which an upcoming event is discussed. Be sure to write complete sentences and avoid sentence fragments.

Writing Tip

Remember to use **relative pronouns** (*who, whom, whose, which, that*) in dependent clauses. Use **interrogative pronouns** (*who, whom, whose, which, what*) in questions.

Dependent Clause: *who arrived late*
  My sister, *who arrived late*, was surprised.
Question: *Who arrived late?*

JOINING SENTENCES

THINK ABOUT

For variety in your writing, you can join two independent clauses to form a *compound sentence*.

Aunt Ruth bought me a plaid scarf. She gave it to me for my birthday.

Aunt Ruth bought me a plaid scarf, *and* she gave it to me for my birthday.

You can also join two independent clauses to form a **complex sentence** if you turn one independent clause into a dependent clause. Remember to use a **comma** after a **dependent clause** that introduces a sentence. To change one independent clause into a dependent clause, add a **subordinating conjunction**. The following subordinating conjunctions show a variety of relationships between clauses.

Subordinating Conjunctions

Time:	after, as, as soon as, before, once, since, until, when, whenever, while
Place:	where, wherever
Cause/Effect:	because, since, in order that, so that
Conditional:	although, even, if, unless, whether

The following are **complex sentences** formed with **subordinating conjunctions.**

- Ron reached the cabin. It grew dark.
  Ron reached the cabin *before* it grew dark.

- Danya was late. She missed the bus.
  Because Danya was late, she missed the bus.

- We posted signs everywhere. We never found our dog.
  Although we posted signs everywhere, we never found our dog.

You can also change an independent clause into a dependent clause by adding a **relative pronoun** (*who, whom, whose, which,* or *that*). Remember to use **commas** to set off a **dependent clause** that is not essential to the meaning of the sentence.

The following are **complex sentences** formed with **relative pronouns**.

- Miranda is a track star. She wins tough races.
  Miranda is a track star *who* wins tough races.

- Dr. Chu works at the clinic. Patients trust him.
  Dr. Chu, *whom* patients trust, works at the clinic.

- This puzzle is easy. It comes with directions.
  This puzzle, *which* comes with directions, is easy.

STUDY A MODEL

Read these babysitting tips for teens.

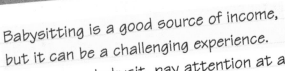

Babysitting is a good source of income, but it can be a challenging experience.
- When you babysit, pay attention at all times. Don't get distracted.
- Even if a home is baby-proofed, be aware. Clean up wherever babies play. Put away small objects because babies can choke on them.
- Ask for contact numbers that you can call in an emergency. Give your parents the address where you will be and the name of the person who hired you.
- Bring toys that will entertain children.

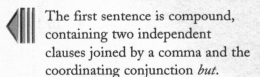
Subordinating conjunctions are red, and relative pronouns are blue.

The first sentence is compound, containing two independent clauses joined by a comma and the coordinating conjunction *but*.

The second, fourth, fifth, sixth, seventh, and eighth sentences are all complex. In the fifth sentence, the dependent clause begins with the subordinating conjunction *because*.

The seventh sentence contains the subordinating conjunction *where* and the relative pronoun *who*.

PRACTICE

A *Read each dependent clause. Label it S if it has a subordinating conjunction or R if it has a relative pronoun.*

1. whenever the shipment arrives
2. who had a foreign accent
3. where the routes intersect
4. whose mother is an accountant
5. whom Naomi met last week
6. which uses less gasoline
7. because diamonds are valuable
8. whether the team captain can play

B *Read each complex sentence. Write the subordinating conjunction and label it S, or write the relative pronoun and label it R.*

1. Chrissy threw away the sandwich because the bread was moldy.
2. Chet, who is ill with the flu, missed practice.
3. Apply polish wherever the leather is worn and cracked.
4. The guide conducted a tour that was lively and informative.
5. Rents have skyrocketed since the area became popular.
6. Study hall, which is held in a classroom, is quiet.
7. A cousin whom I have never met lives in Vietnam.
8. Although the restaurant was crowded, we were seated quickly.

C *Read the paragraph. Rewrite it, joining sentences that express related ideas. Form at least 1 compound sentence and 2 complex sentences. Use underlining for italics.*

William S. Gilbert was a British playwright. He worked with the composer Arthur Sullivan. Together the two men produced more than a dozen comic operas in the late 1800s. These comic operas included *The Mikado, The Pirates of Penzance,* and *H.M.S. Pinafore.* The satirical lyrics often poked fun at Victorian ideals. The lyrics included ingenious rhymes. American theater companies produced the musicals without paying for their use. Gilbert and Sullivan came to the United States in 1879 to protect their copyrights. Gilbert and Sullivan became famous through their musical collaboration. They ended their 25-year partnership in 1896. Gilbert and Sullivan's operettas were popular in England. Both men were knighted.

For sentence variety, you can sometimes join two independent clauses to form a **complex sentence** by changing one independent clause into a dependent clause starting with a **subordinating conjunction** or a **relative pronoun**.

WRITE

Write your own babysitting tips or write tips telling how best to perform a certain job, sport, hobby, or task. Use complex sentences to add variety to your writing.

Writing Tip

Some words can be either a **subordinating conjunction** or a **preposition**, depending on their use.

Subordinating Conjunctions	Prepositions
after I finish	after the movie
before they leave	before noon
since we won	since vacation
until he eats	until tomorrow

THINK ABOUT

To avoid writing a series of short, choppy, repetitive sentences, you can join two related independent clauses by making one clause an appositive. An **appositive** is a word or a phrase that identifies or renames another noun or pronoun.

The tour is at its last stop. The stop is Lynch Castle.

The tour is at its last stop, **Lynch Castle**.

Salsa is my favorite snack food. Salsa is spicy.
*Salsa, **my favorite snack food**, is spicy.*

Roy is a skilled mechanic. Roy restored a classic car.
*Roy, **a skilled mechanic**, restored a classic car.*

An appositive cannot stand alone as a sentence because it does not express a complete thought.
Incorrect: A large city hospital.
Correct: Sid is at St. Jude, *a large city hospital.*

- Use a **comma** or **commas** to separate an appositive from the rest of the sentence if the appositive is not essential and could be removed without changing the basic meaning of the sentence.

    My sister, *Alana*, brought homemade cherry pie.
    (The writer has only one sister, so naming the sister is not essential.)
    The Forum, *a sturdy structure*, still stands.
    (The added detail is not essential.)
    Matsuo Basho, *a Japanese poet*, wrote haiku.
    Have you ever eaten mahi-mahi, *a type of fish*?
    Omri has one hobby, *photography*.

- Do not use a **comma** or **commas** with an appositive that is essential to the meaning of the word that it identifies or renames.

    My sister *Alana* brought homemade cherry pie.
    (The writer has more than one sister, so it is essential to name the sister.)

    Kenji is learning the Japanese martial art *karate*.
    (The detail is needed to tell which martial art Kenji is learning.)

    The tropical fish *mahi-mahi* can be grilled.
    Omri admires the photographer *Edward Weston*.

STUDY A MODEL

Read this entry from a travel guide.

Angkor Wat, the largest religious structure in the world, is in Cambodia. The vast temple was built between 1113 and 1150 and was dedicated to the Hindu god Vishnu. The temple has five towers, which represent the five peaks of Mount Meru. This mountain is the home of the Hindu gods. Angkor Wat also has the world's longest bas-relief, an elaborately carved wall. Angkor Wat, a popular tourist site, was hidden in the jungle for centuries until the naturalist Henri Mouchot uncovered it in 1860.

The appositives are red.

Commas are used around the appositive *the largest religious structure in the world,* which identifies the noun *Angkor Wat.*

Do not confuse other kinds of modifiers with appositives. The adjective clause *which represent the five peaks of Mount Meru* is not an appositive; it does not rename.

A popular tourist site is an appositive that explains the noun *Angkor Wat.*

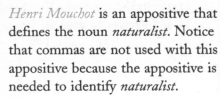

Henri Mouchot is an appositive that defines the noun *naturalist.* Notice that commas are not used with this appositive because the appositive is needed to identify *naturalist.*

PRACTICE

A *Read each sentence. Write the appositive phrase. If there is no appositive phrase, write None.*

1. Tracey, a nurse at General Hospital, takes care of sick infants.
2. Dessert will be *gelato*, which is Italian ice cream.
3. I heard a piece by Erik Satie, my favorite composer.
4. Mount Rainier is a volcanic mountain in Washington.
5. Kate, an experienced editor, corrects most mistakes.
6. Everyone looks forward to the Lilac Ball, an annual event.
7. Dan, who enjoys winter sports, bought cross-country skis.
8. Amelia Earhart, an American aviator, set several records.

B *Join each pair of sentences, using the underlined words as an appositive phrase. Use commas correctly.*

1. Mr. Dalton is <u>a respected scholar</u>. Mr. Dalton offered his opinion.
2. Peggy bought a jar of cardamom. Cardamom is <u>a fragrant spice</u>.
3. Lea enjoys <u>her newest hobby</u>. Lea's newest hobby is sketching.
4. Acid rain is <u>an environmental threat</u>. Acid rain is caused by pollution.
5. At the audition, Rod sang "<u>Over There</u>." "Over There" is a patriotic song.
6. Is gazpacho easy to prepare? Gazpacho is <u>a cold soup</u>.
7. René Magritte was <u>a surrealist painter</u>. René Magritte was born in Belgium.
8. Chandra wears a sari. A sari is <u>a garment from India</u>.

C *Read the paragraph. Rewrite it, joining each pair of related sentences to form a sentence that includes an appositive. Use commas correctly. Use underlining for italics.*

The hummingbird is the world's smallest bird. The hummingbird is both colorful and fast. Spanish explorers called these rainbowlike birds *Joyas voladoras*. The Spanish words *Joyas voladoras* mean "flying jewels." The hummingbird is a tiny powerhouse. It can fly forward, backward, and sideways and can reach speeds of 60 miles per hour. The sun gem is a South American hummingbird. The sun gem beats its wings 90 times per second! For energy, hummingbirds daily consume half their weight in nectar. Nectar is the sweet liquid produced by flowers.

For sentence variety, you can sometimes join two related independent clauses by changing one clause to an appositive. An **appositive** is a word or phrase that identifies or renames a noun or pronoun in the same sentence.

WRITE

Write an entry for a travel guide, describing a building, park, or other point of interest that you are familiar with. Use appositives to vary the sentences in your description.

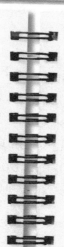

Writing Tip

You can join **simple sentences and complex sentences** by making one independent clause an appositive.

Simple: Walter is my neighbor.

Complex: Walter walks his dog when he gets home at night.

Joined: Walter, my neighbor, walks his dog when he gets home at night.

RUN-ON AND RAMBLING SENTENCES

THINK ABOUT

Avoid confusing your readers with unclear sentences. A **run-on sentence** consists of two or more separate complete thoughts that run together without correct punctuation. A **rambling sentence** has too many complete thoughts joined by conjunctions such as *and*, *but*, or *so*, without correct punctuation.

- One way to correct a **run-on sentence** is to use a *period*, *question mark*, or *exclamation point* to make separate simple sentences.

  Run-on Sentence: The candle flickers a drop of wax falls.
  Correct: The candle flickers. A drop of wax falls.

  Run-on Sentence: Does Al have a map we're lost.
  Correct: Does Al have a map? We're lost.

  Run-on Sentence: I can't believe it you're on time.
  Correct: I can't believe it! You're on time.

- Another way to correct a **run-on sentence** is to create a **compound sentence** by using a *comma* and a *conjunction* such as *and*, *but*, or *or*. Or you can use a *semicolon*.

  Run-on Sentence: The wolf snarled it ran off.
  Correct: The wolf snarled, **and** it ran off.
  Correct: The wolf snarled; it ran off.

  Run-on Sentence: Chad eats grits I like oatmeal.
  Correct: Chad eats grits, **but** I like oatmeal.
  Correct: Chad eats grits; I like oatmeal.

- Correct a **rambling sentence** by creating separate sentences (simple, compound, or complex). Use appropriate connecting words and punctuation.

  Rambling Sentence: Tess loves to eat but she hates to cook so she often eats in diners or she gets take-out food.
  Correct: Tess loves to eat, but she hates to cook. She often eats in diners, or she gets take-out food. (2 compound sentences)
  Correct: Tess loves to eat. Since she hates to cook, she often eats in diners or gets take-out food. (1 simple sentence, 1 complex sentence)

STUDY A MODEL

Read the draft and the edit of a class trip itinerary.

draft: We'll meet at the station on Friday morning so we'll take the 8:05 train and we'll arrive in the city at 9:30 A.M. Then we'll proceed to the art museum the guard will meet us in the lobby. Don't wander off the tour will begin on time.

edit: We'll meet at the station on Friday morning. We'll take the 8:05 train, and we'll arrive in the city at 9:30 A.M. Then we'll proceed to the art museum; the guard will meet us in the lobby. Don't wander off! The tour will begin on time.

Run-on sentences are red, and rambling sentences are blue.

In the draft, the first sentence is rambling. It has three separate complete thoughts joined together with the conjunctions *so* and *and*. In the edit, the sentence has been broken into a simple sentence and a compound sentence. In the compound sentences, the independent clauses are joined by a comma and the conjunction *and*.

In the draft, the second and third sentences are run-on. In the edit, the first run-on is made into a compound sentence by adding a semicolon. The second run-on is split into two separate sentences, with appropriate punctuation and capitalization.

PRACTICE

A *Read each sentence. Label it* **Run-on** *or* **Rambling**.

1. Who wrote that lyrical piece of music it sounds like Brahms.
2. A guide gave him maps and Wes started hiking but stopped.
3. The shirt fit her perfectly she didn't like the mango color.
4. This book was fascinating but it was very long and I had trouble finishing it.
5. Look out the park bench has just been painted bright green.
6. Squirrels gather acorns or they devour birdseed and they like plant bulbs.

B *Read the sentences. Rewrite each run-on sentence as a compound sentence, using the clues in parentheses. Rewrite each rambling sentence as two separate sentences, with correct punctuation. Try to create at least 1 complex sentence.*

1. The hurricane pounded the coast Miami was flooded. (comma + *and*)
2. Please help me the assignment is extremely confusing. (semicolon)
3. Carrie has a poodle but she also likes cats and she wants a gerbil.
4. That tire was almost flat Chad filled it with air. (comma + *so*)
5. Hot-air balloons filled the sky no one stopped to watch. (comma + *but*)
6. The bus stopped but then it sped away so the commuters were stranded.
7. Those videos are entertaining and the comedies are fun but I prefer the dramas.

C *Read the paragraph. Rewrite it, correcting the run-on and rambling sentences.*

At the beginning of the 19th century, there were no corner newsstands so newspapers were not readily available and few ordinary citizens read the news. Newspapers were sold only by subscription it cost between 8 and 12 dollars a year to subscribe. The average worker made about a dollar a day so many people could not afford a subscription and mostly wealthy politicians and industrialists bought newspapers. By the middle of the 1800s, publishers appealed to a wider audience newsboys sold papers to the general public and this reduced the cost.

> Correct **run-on sentences** or **rambling sentences** by creating separate sentences (simple, compound, or complex). Use appropriate capitalization, punctuation, and connecting words.

WRITE

Write about a class trip you have taken. Check your writing for any run-on or rambling sentences. If you find any, correct them.

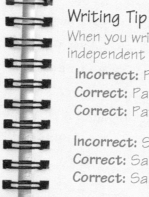

Writing Tip

When you write, do not use a comma to join independent clauses (simple sentences).

Incorrect: Pat studies, she gets As.
Correct: Pat studies; she gets As.
Correct: Pat studies, and she gets As.

Incorrect: Sam fell, then he cried.
Correct: Sam fell; then he cried.
Correct: Sam fell, and then he cried.

REVISING SENTENCES

THINK ABOUT

Revising sentences can greatly improve your writing. When you revise, make sure that *sentence structures* are parallel and that *verb tenses* are consistent. Also, *delete weak or unnecessary words or ideas.*

- Use **parallel structure**. Make sure that similar parts of a sentence are the same part of speech or have the same construction.

  Not Parallel: Jane *likes drama* and *to read* mysteries.
  Parallel: Jane *likes drama* and *mysteries.*

  Not Parallel: Gerard skates *skillfully* and *rapid.*
  Parallel: Gerard skates *skillfully* and *rapidly.*

  Not Parallel: Alexis *is an English teacher* and *tutoring math.*
  Parallel: Alexis *teaches English* and *tutors math.*
  Parallel: Alexis *is an English teacher* and *a math tutor.*

- Make **verb tenses consistent**. Don't shift tenses unless the time of the action differs.
  Incorrect: Juan *fishes*, and Ray *rowed* the boat.
  Correct: Juan *fishes*, and Ray *rows* the boat.
  Correct: Juan *fished*, and Ray *rowed* the boat.

- Delete **unnecessary or weak words and phrases**.
  Weak: This *wet rain* is good for the lawn. (Rain is wet, so the word *wet* is unnecessary.)
  Better: This *rain* is good for the lawn.

  Weak: *In view of the fact that* I felt ill, I left.
  Better: *Because* I felt ill, I left.

  Weak: *This here twig* is actually an insect!
  Better: *This twig* is actually an insect!

  Weak: *What I mean is* the theater is crowded.
  Better: The theater is crowded.

  Weak: Cy takes a *daily* walk *every day.*
  Better: Cy takes a *daily* walk.
  Better: Cy takes a walk *every day.*

  Weak: An *animal went* up a *tree*. (Use precise nouns and verbs when possible.)
  Better: A *squirrel scampered* up a *gnarled maple.*

STUDY A MODEL

Read the draft and edit of a block party notice.

draft: Neighbors in our neighborhood will hold a block party on June 2. Come to share food and playing games. Secor Street will be blocked off on account of the fact that we obtained a permit. Bring food and something else to eat and to provide chairs. Come to this here event!

edit: Our neighborhood will hold a block party on June 2. Come to share food and to play games. Secor Street will be blocked off because we obtained a permit. Bring food and extra chairs. Come to this event!

Words and phrases that need revision are red.

 In the first sentence of the draft, the words *Neighbors* and *neighborhood* are both unnecessary.

 The structure of the second sentence is not parallel. *To share food* and *playing games* are not the same construction.

 In the edited version, the unnecessary words *on account of the fact that* have been changed to *because.* Other unnecessary or weak words or phases have been deleted or replaced.

PRACTICE

A *Read each sentence. Rewrite it, deleting any unnecessary words and phrases.*

1. Gallagher suddenly collapsed on the hard pavement.
2. The class was silent during the time of the exam.
3. Where has my bright yellow canary gone to?
4. The carpenters they pounded the nails with a hammer.
5. Is that there melon a honeydew or a cantaloupe?
6. The three triplets do not dress alike.
7. Because of the fact that she was hungry, Lorna ate a snack.

B *Read each sentence. Rewrite it, correcting errors in structure or verb tense.*

1. That celebrity is a singer and acts in plays.
2. Frances looked at her watch and stares out the window.
3. The bell will ring, and the students have left.
4. I will wallpaper my room, and I have painted the trim.
5. Sumi listened to the speech and is applauding politely.
6. The late-day mail is delivered in the afternoon by a mail carrier.
7. Do the floorboards creak when you crept up the staircase?

C *Read the paragraph. Rewrite it, making sentence elements parallel, correcting inconsistent verb tenses, and eliminating any weak or unnecessary words or phrases.*

Meteorologists analyze data and made weather forecasts. Typically they usually give updates about weather conditions periodically every so often. Good weather forecasters use state-of-the-art equipment to make predictions about what will happen. They consult the national weather wire, weather radar screens, and are using current-surface map machines. Forecasters use data that they collect and gather to determine weather patterns around the country in the United States. Most people are interested in weather changes in view of the fact that we are all of us affected by the temperature and by rain or snowing.

Revise sentences to correct structure or verb tense and to delete unnecessary or weak words or phrases.

WRITE

Write the draft of a notice that you might post in your school or neighborhood. Then edit the sentences to improve word choices and to eliminate any errors in sentence structure and verb tense.

Writing Tip

Whenever possible, use the **active voice** to make your writing more forceful.

Passive: The late train is often taken by weary commuters.

Active: Weary commuters often take the late train.

Passive: I was counseled in a supportive way by my favorite supervisor.

Active: My favorite supervisor counseled me in a supportive way.

43

VARYING SENTENCES

THINK ABOUT

Varying sentences makes your writing more effective. You can add variety by changing the **structure**, the **length**, or the **type** of sentences you use.

- **Vary the beginnings of sentences.** Begin some sentences with a **modifier**.

    Finally the storm was over.
    From the north, the riders galloped into town.
    Hobbling on crutches, Cia slowly went upstairs.
    To pass the law, the legislators met all night.
    Though he went to the mall, Leo bought nothing.
    With intensity, our instructor stressed safety.

- For variety, occasionally change the normal **order of words** in a sentence, putting the verb before the subject.

    An old *well* **stood** behind the shed.
    Behind the shed **stood** an old *well*.

    A veteran *pilot* **is flying** the plane.
    Flying the plane **is** a veteran *pilot*.

- **Vary the length and type of sentences.**
- Use a combination of short and longer *simple, compound,* and *complex* sentences.

    Ben owns a used-book store. He sometimes sells rare books. (simple sentences)
    Ben owns a used-book store, and he sometimes sells rare books. (compound sentence)
    Because Ben owns a used-book store, he sometimes sells rare books. (complex sentence)

- Create some sentences with *compound subjects* or *compound predicates.*

    Chelsea applauded for Louise.
    Lee applauded for Louise.
    ┌compound subject┐
    Chelsea and Lee applauded for Louise.

    The snake hissed at us.
    The snake then slithered away.
    └──────compound predicate──────┘
    The snake *hissed at us and then slithered away.*

STUDY A MODEL

Read this part of a script for a documentary film.

The camera focuses on a bush and moves in for a close up. Among the green leaves is a praying mantis. It clings stick-like to a slender twig. A butterfly, a cricket, and a katydid flit into view. Which will be the next victim? While the music builds ominously, the camera zooms in on the mantis. In silence, the insect watches its prey. The stalker remains perfectly still. Suddenly the mantis lunges; the katydid becomes a tasty meal.

> *Notice the variety in the structure, length, and type of sentences.*

The normal order of words (*A praying mantis is among the green leaves*) has been inverted to add variety.

Notice the simple sentence with the compound subject: *A butterfly, a cricket, and a katydid.*

Notice that using an interrogative sentence (*Which will be the next victim?*) adds interest by breaking up a series of declarative sentences.

The last sentence is compound, with two independent clauses joined by a semicolon. This sentence begins with the adverb *Suddenly.*

PRACTICE

A *Read each sentence. Rewrite it to begin with the underlined modifier. Use appropriate punctuation.*

1. You can see that asteroid belt <u>with a powerful telescope</u>.
2. Jude signed a petition <u>to protest the mayor's decision</u>.
3. Robin spoke persuasively <u>during the book discussion</u>.
4. Mr. Vanderwicke, <u>smiling humbly</u>, accepted his degree.
5. Gayle sketched the intricate design <u>carefully and skillfully</u>.
6. A tourist, <u>inspired by the views</u>, paused by the window.
7. Amber tackled the difficult task <u>after she had rested</u>.
8. The hikers, <u>taking their time</u>, scaled the ridge.

B *Combine each pair of sentences to form one simple sentence with a compound subject or a compound predicate.*

1. Carl joined the league. Tim joined the league.
2. The driver stopped the bus. The driver opened the door.
3. I ran fast. I finally got home.
4. Tessa entered a project in the science fair. I entered a project in the science fair.

C *Read the paragraph. Rewrite it, adding more variety by changing the structure, length, or type of several sentences.*

The Amazon River Basin in South America is a tropical rain forest. It is home to an amazing diversity of plants and animals. A green wall of evergreens grows along the river bank. Ferns and orchids hang from boughs. Dense foliage shades the forest from the hot sun. Different kinds of animals live in the rain forest. Jaguars and leopards, prowling for food, live on the ground. Screeching parrots live in the tree canopy. Chattering monkeys live in the tree canopy. Many kinds of snakes and insects climb in the trees. Many kinds of snakes and insects crawl on the ground.

Add variety to your writing by changing the **structure**, **length**, or **type** of sentences that you use.

WRITE

Imagine that your life will be the subject of a documentary film. Describe one scene from the film, varying the structure, type, and length of sentences.

Writing Tip
To add emphasis, you can sometimes use single words or phrases in your writing.
Good job!
Excellent!
No way!
Never happen.
Yes!
Help!

45

CAPITALIZATION: PEOPLE

THINK ABOUT

Capitalize the **first names** and **last names** and **initials** of **specific people**.

Sara **D**emic	Jane **O**tis **S**mith
Austin **P**owers	Nina **P**enfield-**P**aine
Eddie **M**oney	**E. B. W**hite
John **B. G**oode	**A. L**ouise **H**osmer

- Capitalize **titles** and **abbreviated titles** used with names of specific people.

President **E**isenhower	**D**r. Yul **B. B**etter
Mayor **D**olan	**M**rs. Lombardi
Principal McCann	**E. E.** Curley, **J**r.
Queen Elizabeth	Lea Cafieri, **P**h.**D**.

Mr. Johnson is my favorite teacher.
Have you read the works of *J. R. R. Tolkien*?
My friends go *Dr. C. Englender*.
Abe has an appointment with *Professor Gilmore*.
Read the publication of *J. Aquiles Sanchez, Ph.D.*

- Capitalize a **title** or a **family name** when it is used in place of a name or as part of name.

We'll be careful, *Officer*.
Hurry, *Uncle*, or you'll be late.
I called *Father* with the news.
Aunt Fay is not at home.
Did *Mayor Fernandez* call?

- Do not capitalize a title or a family name when it is *not* used to take the place of a name or when it is not used as part of a specific name.

The *officer* spoke softly.
My *uncle* is always late.
Did your *dad* hear the news?
The *mayor* will call.

- Capitalize the names of **groups of people** from cities, states, regions, countries, and continents.

Philadelphians	**S**outherners
Nebraskans	**C**anadians

LeAnn is a native *Missourian*.
Edmund, a *Belgian*, speaks several languages.

STUDY A MODEL

Read this memo.

To: All Staff   Date: January 12, 2004
From: V. Lee   Subject: Meeting Agenda
- The conference with the Germans visiting our facility will be tomorrow.
- Chief Executive Officer Jeb D. Pruitt will report on his meeting with a group of Parisians at our lab in France.
- Mr. T. D. O'Riley will discuss negotiations with the Californians who want to join our research team.
- The meeting set up by Dr. Seymour and another doctor with the South Americans has been postponed.

The title *Chief Executive Officer* is capitalized because it is used as part of a specific person's name. *Jeb D. Pruitt* is capitalized because it is a specific person's name.

Notice that the title, the initials, and both parts of the last name are capitalized in *Mr. T. D. O'Riley*.

Notice that the abbreviation for *doctor* (*Dr.*) is capitalized, but the word *doctor* is not capitalized because it is not used as part of a specific name.

46

PRACTICE

A *Write each item correctly.*

1. detective rich tracy
2. berliners
3. judge may b. fair
4. spaniards
5. j. a. macey, r.n.
6. mayor mai chang
7. dan's cousin
8. r. j. rosenberg, jr.

B *Read each sentence. Find the word or words that should be capitalized and write them correctly. If there are no errors, write **Correct**.*

1. I surprised my grandmother at her 80th birthday party.
2. An italian from Milan won the prize.
3. When did sergeant walker report for duty?
4. A couple of new yorkers invented a delicious sandwich.
5. He is fascinated by the dialect of the lifelong new englanders.
6. My parents have an appointment with the principal.
7. In 1910, otis fingerling, sr., immigrated to the United States.
8. Veteran sprinter marilyn c. smith captured first place.

C *Read the paragraph. Find the 8 words or names that should be capitalized and write them correctly.*

My brother, a native californian, lives in a college dormitory with students from many nations. He often sends mother newsy emails. His roommate is a norwegian who speaks four languages. His favorite class, taught by dr. w. b. singer, is about europeans in the 1400s. For parties, the three southwesterners in the dorm prepare spicy foods. My brother writes that dr. phil o. sofer, his faculty advisor, encourages him to learn about different cultures. My brother's dorm counselor, one of two chicagoans in the dorm, helped a couple of freshmen from foreign countries get over their initial homesickness.

> **Capitalize** people's names and initials, titles, abbreviated titles, and words used as names. Also capitalize the names of groups of people from cities, states, regions, countries, and continents.

WRITE

Write a memo about a family, school, or community meeting that you wish would take place. Include initials, titles, or abbreviated titles, if appropriate. Make sure to capitalize each name correctly.

Writing Tip

Always capitalize the personal pronoun *I*, alone or in a contraction.

I like a big breakfast.

I sleep better if I've exercised during the day.

I'll let you know when he and I are ready.

I'd like to receive a call three minutes before I'm on.

CAPITALIZATION: PLACES

THINK ABOUT

Capitalize the names of **specific places**, such as the following.

Cities:	New Orleans, Addis Ababa, Edinburgh
States:	South Carolina, Missouri, Oklahoma
Provinces:	Ontario, Hunan, Yukon Territory
Regions:	Mid-Atlantic States, Provence, Middle East
Countries:	Tanzania, Costa Rica, Spain
Continents:	South America, Antarctica, Africa
Planets:	Mercury, Pluto, Saturn
Roadways:	Park Avenue, Garden State Parkway, Champs Élysées
Landforms:	Grand Canyon, Niagara Falls, Colorado Plateau
Deserts:	Sahara, Kalahari Desert, Gobi Desert
Mountains:	White Mountains, Atlas Mountains, the Himalayas
Bodies of Water:	Bering Sea, Atlantic Ocean, Mississippi River, Lake Michigan
Islands:	St. Thomas, Puerto Rico, Marshall Islands
Parks:	Lincoln Park, Rajaji National Park, Amboseli National Park
Buildings:	Sears Tower, Parthenon, Jefferson High School
Landmarks:	Alamo, Eiffel Tower, Angkor Wat
Bridges:	Golden Gate Bridge, Rialto Bridge, Verrazano-Narrows Bridge

Capitalize **directional words** when they name *regions*. Do not capitalize these words when they give *directions*.

> The *South* is known for its hot weather. (region)
> We live just *south* of the school. (direction)
> Did he grow up in the *Northwest*? (region)
> Did you go *northwest* toward the freeway? (direction)

STUDY A MODEL

Read this entry from Amy's travel journal.

Tuesday, June 28
   Today I arrived in Dublin, Ireland. In the morning, I took a bus to Phoenix Park and went to the zoo. Later, I strolled across Ha'penny Bridge over the River Liffey. The river was smaller than I had imagined! Then I ate lunch and shopped on Grafton Street. This afternoon, I saw the General Post Office on O'Connell Street where Irish nationalists and British soldiers fought in the early 1900s. Tomorrow I'll visit Trinity College to see the Book of Kells. In just two days, I'll be flying back to Montana.

Place names are red.

 Dublin and *Ireland* name a specific city and country and are capitalized.

Notice that *zoo* is not capitalized. It is not part of a name of a specific zoo.

 The word *River* in *River Liffey* is capitalized because it is part of the name of a specific river. In the next sentence, the word *river* is not capitalized because it does not name a specific river.

 Trinity College and *Montana* name specific places.

PRACTICE

A *Read the sentences. Write the 12 names of specific places.*

1. My family took pictures of Mauna Loa in Hawaii.
2. What do scientists know about Venus and Mars?
3. What a photo you took of Victoria Falls on the Zambesi River!
4. Have you ever visited the Space Needle in Seattle?
5. Take Interstate 95 to the Baltimore Harbor Tunnel.
6. Darren explored Arches National Park in Utah.

B *Read each phrase. Capitalize the words that should be capitalized.*

1. touring british columbia
2. eating new england clam chowder
3. climbing pike's peak
4. collecting shells on sanibel island
5. visiting the uffizi gallery
6. photographing the washington monument
7. jogging in central park
8. looking at a map of asia

C *Read the paragraph. Find the 10 place names that should be capitalized and write them correctly.*

Beryl Markham (1902–1986), a female aviator, grew up on a horse farm near nairobi, kenya. As a young woman, she trained horses and became a commercial pilot. Markham delivered goods, passengers, and mail to isolated regions of the country. In 1936, she attempted a record-breaking solo flight east to west across the atlantic ocean from london to new york. Flying against the wind without a radio, she piloted a single-engine plane from europe to north america. After a fuel line froze, Markham had to crash land in a peat bog in nova scotia, but she instantly became a celebrity. Markham later briefly lived in california, where she ran an avocado ranch, but she spent most of her life in eastern africa.

Capitalize the names of **places,** and capitalize **directional words** when they name regions.

WRITE

Write a travel journal entry for an area you have visited or for your own city or town. Include the names of parks, buildings, landforms, or other sights that you think are interesting. Capitalize each place name correctly.

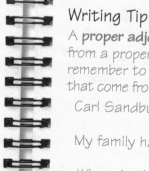

Writing Tip

A **proper adjective** is an adjective formed from a proper noun. When you write, remember to capitalize proper adjectives that come from names of specific places.

Carl Sandburg was a Midwestern poet.

My family has Scottish roots.

Where is the best Asian market in the city?

CAPITALIZATION: THINGS

THINK ABOUT

Capitalize the names of **specific things**, such as the following:

Holidays:	Memorial Day, Thanksgiving
Days of Week:	Wednesday, Saturday, Monday
Months:	October, May, August
Historical Periods:	Middle Ages, Renaissance, Great Depression
Special Events:	Westminster Dog Show, Olympics
Works of Art:	*The Man with the Blue Guitar, The Thinker*
Books:	*The Once and Future King, I Know Why the Caged Bird Sings, A Wrinkle in Time*
Poems:	"The Old Clock on the Stairs," "The Raven"
Songs:	"America the Beautiful"
Plays:	*Twelfth Night*
Newspapers:	*Sacramento Bee, Washington Post*
Magazines:	*Cobblestone, National Geographic Kids, Time for Kids*
Forms of Transportation:	Boston and Maine Railroad, U.S.S. *Constitution, Mir*

Brand Names:	Slippon shoes, Lotsa Crunch cereal, Dazzle detergent (The type of product is not capitalized.)
Government Groups:	Supreme Court, House of Representatives, Department of the Interior
Companies:	Bright Paint Company, Techtron Corporation, Dee's Sporting Goods, Inc.
Organizations:	Boy Scouts, Parent Teacher Association, Organization of American States
Institutions:	Fairfax County Public Library, University of Florida, Highlands Baptist Church
Clubs:	Quilting Guild, Taconic Postcard Club, Seattle Windsurfing Club
Teams:	Beacon Badgers, Pocono Piranhas, Lewiston Lions
Languages:	German, Swedish, Bengali
Groups:	Asians, Native Americans, Caucasians
Nationalities:	Mexican, Polish, Japanese
Religions:	Christianity, Buddhism, Islam

STUDY A MODEL

Read this advertisement.

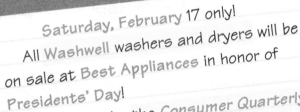

Saturday, February 17 only!
All Washwell washers and dryers will be on sale at Best Appliances in honor of Presidents' Day!
Come see why the Consumer Quarterly rates these washers and dryers #1. Watch the members of the Vail Bowling Club demonstrate the cleaning power of these machines as they wash their own bowling shirts! Save even more—look for our special discount coupons in the Middletown News.
Open 8 to 8! Take Route 17, Exit 5.
Metro Transit, #55, to third stop.

Names of specific things are red.

The common nouns *washers* and *dryers*, following the capitalized brand name *Washwell,* are not capitalized.

In titles such as *Consumer Quarterly,* the first and last words and other important words are capitalized. (Articles *[a, an, the],* short conjunctions, and short prepositions are not capitalized unless they are the first or the last word.) Here, the article *the* is not capitalized because it is not part of the title.

Middletown News is the name of a specific newspaper. The article *the* is not capitalized because it is not part of the name of the paper.

PRACTICE

A *Read each phrase. Write correctly the words that should be capitalized. If there are no errors, write* **Correct.** *Use underlining for italics.*

1. flying on atlantic airways
2. eating Cheesies
3. celebrating thanksgiving
4. studying the tang dynasty
5. listening to "Stars and Stripes Forever"
6. working with Carl at pete's delicatessen
7. riding on *explorer I*
8. reading *Jazz-Riffs* magazine with Rachel

B *Read each sentence. Find the words that should be capitalized and write them correctly. Use underlining for italics.*

1. My brother played a prank on april fool's day.
2. What effects did the industrial revolution have on our society?
3. A salesman from mighty mousetrap company won the raffle.
4. The bill was passed by a majority of congress.
5. The twins will come home on sunday.
6. Buy a freshaire fan to be cool this summer!
7. I left my copy of *the good earth* on the bus.
8. Holly often studies at shawsheen public library.

C *Read the paragraph. Find the 8 names of specific things that should be capitalized and write them correctly. Use underlining for italics.*

On wednesday, the newtown art club took a trip to the heard museum in Phoenix, Arizona. The club chose this museum because *usa today* called it "the nation's most prestigious private indian arts center." The president of the art club, Betty Fitzsimmons, arranged the trip during a hoop dance contest that is held every february. The group also enjoyed looking at the fine collection of native american art. One member of the club, Paula Kaye, especially liked *seaweed people*, a bronze sculpture by artist John Hoover.

Capitalize the names of most **specific things**.

WRITE

Write an advertisement for some things that you own and would like to sell. Make sure to capitalize names of specific things correctly.

Writing Tip

Do not capitalize **seasons** or **centuries** unless they are part of a name or title.

This spring I will visit Nana.
Are you going to the Spring Fling?

I was born during the twentieth century.
The Women of the Twentieth Century is a great reference book.

THINK ABOUT

Using **commas** to separate, or set off, various elements can make your writing easier to understand.

- Use a **comma** to separate items in **addresses** and **dates**.

    Sioux City, Nebraska   July 4, 1776

    If the address or date is in a sentence, use a **comma** after the state or after the year.

    The exhibit opens in Utica, *New York,* on February 5, *2004,* at the Proctor Arts Institute.

- Use a **comma** after the **greeting** in a friendly letter and after the **closing** in any letter.

    Dear Anna, (greeting)   Sincerely, (closing)

- Use a **comma** to separate two or more **adjectives** that equally describe the same **noun**.

    It was a *muddy, rutty* track.
    How much is this *delicate, ornate* vase?

- Use **commas** with **introductory words** such as *first, well,* or *yes,* and with nouns of **direct address**.

    First, peel the sweet potatoes.
    Yes, that's a good idea. *Well,* I agree.
    Your sweet potato pie, *Lily,* wins first prize.
    Will you meet me after school, *Matt?*

- Use **commas** to set off a **parenthetical expression**, which interrupts a sentence.

    The movie, *in my opinion,* was too long.
    Nicole, *of course,* was late.

- Use a **comma** after a **long dependent clause** or **phrase** at the beginning of a sentence.

    During the blizzard last week, our lights flickered.
    Raging into the night, the storm did not weaken.
    As predicted by Channel 8, the storm lasted for 9 hours.
    Although 16 inches of snow fell, the following day was sunny.

- Remember to use **commas** to set off a **phrase** or **clause** that is *not essential* to the basic meaning of a sentence.

    The center of the team, *7 footer Patrick Wells,* dunked the ball.
    Tom Sims, *who was fouled,* sank his foul shots.
    The final game, *which I missed,* drew a huge crowd.

- Do **not** use **commas** to set off a **phrase** or **clause** that is *essential* to the basic meaning of a sentence.

    The red cup is the one *that I prefer.*
    The point *that made the difference* was yours.
    The coach *who won the game* gave an interview.

STUDY A MODEL

Read this note from Zachary to his friend Skip.

July 18, 2003

Dear Skip,
    Well, friend, here I am in Wells, Maine, visiting James, my favorite cousin. He lives right next to a long, sandy beach. I didn't know that riding the waves, which I'm very good at, could be so much fun! (James, of course, is better.)
    Even though I won't get home until late on Friday, I'll call you with a long, funny story about a fin!

                        Your friend,
                        Zachary

Commas are red.

This comma separates the items in the date.

The greeting in a postcard, similar to a friendly letter, is followed by a comma.

Because the clause *which I'm very good at* is not essential, it is set off with commas.

Of course, a parenthetical phrase, is set off by commas.

The closing of this friendly postcard is followed by a comma.

PRACTICE

A *Write commas correctly in each item.*

1. Dear Grandpa
2. Baltimore Maryland
3. July 14 1976
4. Sincerely yours
5. Dear Mr. Henry
6. Nashua New Hampshire
7. New Year's Day 2005
8. Atlantic City New Jersey
9. Dear Carmen and Hector
10. Cordially yours

B *Read each sentence. Rewrite it, adding the missing commas.*

1. We left Bend Oregon at noon.
2. Steve was born on May 15 1988.
3. Yes I packed a flashlight.
4. I believe Sir Percival that you will win the joust.
5. Benjamin Franklin an American patriot was a printer and inventor.
6. Send this postcard from sunny warm Key West.
7. Despite the deafening noise Joline was able to concentrate.

C *Read the paragraph. Rewrite it, adding the 8 missing commas.*

Thomas A. Edison an American inventor helped change the world of entertainment. Edison patented a motion picture camera which was called a Kinetograph on August 24 1891. Encouraged by the public's interest in moving pictures Edison soon opened a motion picture production studio in West Orange New Jersey. Some of Edison's first silent films showed acts from Buffalo Bill's Wild West Show or scenes of everyday life. At the beginning of the twentieth century Edison's film studio also began to make films that told stories.

Use **commas** to separate or set off various elements to make your writing easier to understand.

WRITE

Write a note to someone you know. Use commas correctly.

Writing Tip
Use a **colon**, not a comma, after the salutation of a business letter.
Dear Miss Shoemaker:
 Please send your most recent catalog showing shoes in extra-wide sizes.
                    Sincerely,
                    Ima Foote

PUNCTUATION: APOSTROPHES

LESSON 26

THINK ABOUT

- Use an **apostrophe** to replace the omitted letter or letters in a **contraction**. A contraction is made by joining a verb with another word.

is not	= *isn't*	who is	= *who's*
does not	= *doesn't*	he would	= *he'd*
cannot	= *can't*	you will	= *you'll*
would not	= *wouldn't*	he will	= *he'll*
he will	= *he'll*	she is	= *she's*
they are	= *they're*	I am	= *I'm*
you have	= *you've*	it is	= *it's*

Who *is not* going to the party?
Who *isn't* going to the party?

I am on my way now.
I'm on my way now.

You will have fun.
You'll have fun!

He would like to bring a gift.
He'd like to bring a gift.

The possessive form shows ownership. Use **apostrophes** to form some **possessives**.

- To form the possessive of a *single noun*, add an apostrophe and *s* (*'s*)
    - the earring of *Tess* *Tess's* earring
    - the collar of the *dog* the *dog's* collar
- To form the possessive of a *plural noun that ends in s*, add only an apostrophe (*'*).
    - rights of *Americans* *Americans'* rights
    - the room of the *twins* the *twins'* room
- To form the possessive of a *plural noun that does not end in s*, add an apostrophe and *s* (*'s*)
    - the toys of the *children* the *children's* toys
    - the flight of the *geese* the *geese's* flight
- Add an apostrophe and *s* (*'s*) to form the possessive of an *indefinite pronoun*.
    - the jacket of *someone* *someone's* jacket
    - the vote of *everybody* *everybody's* vote
- When ownership is shared by *more than one noun*, add an apostrophe and *s* (*'s*) to the last noun in the series.
    - Listen to *Bob and Ray's* ideas. (not Bob's and Ray's)
    - Have you seen the rare *dimes and nickels'* display? (not dimes' and nickels')

STUDY A MODEL

Read this poster for a tag sale.

Apostrophes are red.

GIANT MOVING SALE!
Here's great cheap stuff!
You'll find what you need—don't miss out!
Somebody's junk is another's treasure.
When: July 17–18, 9 to 5. No early birds, please.
Where: 2885 Duck Pond Road
What: Items include the following:
- babies' furniture
- women's and men's clothing
- artist's supplies • gardener's tools
- boys' and girls' sports equipment
- grandma and grandpa's antique china

◄• • In the contraction *Here's*, the apostrophe replaces the letter *i* in the word *is*.

◄• • *Somebody* and *another* are indefinite pronouns. The possessive of these words is formed by adding an apostrophe and *s*.

◄• • *Women* and *men* are plural nouns that don't end in *s*. To show ownership, add an apostrophe and *s* to form *women's* and *men's*.

◄• • Since both grandma and grandpa owned the china, an *s* is added to the last noun, *grandpa*.

54

PRACTICE

A *Read each phrase. Write the possessive form of each underlined noun or pronoun.*

1. the <u>Thompsons</u> lawn
2. <u>no one</u> goggles
3. a <u>sculptor</u> chisel
4. the <u>graduates</u> diplomas
5. the <u>mice</u> cage
6. <u>Beau and Carl</u> sister
7. two <u>oxen</u> yokes
8. <u>one</u> notebook

B *Read each sentence. Rewrite it, adding apostrophes to form possessives or contractions as needed.*

1. Theyll buy lunch at the cafeteria.
2. I left my bag in the womens locker room.
3. The bus doesnt stop here anymore.
4. Neithers tie is colorful.
5. The manager listened to many customers complaints.
6. Hanss watch stopped ticking.
7. Gillian and Lous report was informative.
8. Theyre lost, and its almost time for dinner!

C *Read the paragraph. Rewrite the 11 underlined words and phrases by forming contractions or possessives. Add apostrophes as needed.*

Last summer Debbie worked as a waitress at <u>Joe and Flo</u> Diner, which was originally owned by Sal and Myrna, <u>Flo</u> parents. Debbie <u>had not</u> known how challenging a <u>waitress</u> job could be. Though she <u>did not</u> have any experience, she learned quickly. During the breakfast shift, Debbie quickly discovered that <u>Sal and Myrna</u> Breakfast Delite was the most popular dish. At lunch, Debbie had to remember to hand out <u>children</u> menus and to recite daily specials. When the diner was very busy, all of the waitresses pitched in to serve each <u>other</u> orders. Once tables were empty, Debbie collected <u>customers</u> tips. Above all, she learned the most important rule of food service: <u>Do not</u> forget <u>someone</u> order.

Use **apostrophes** in **contractions** and to form **possessives**.

WRITE

Write a poster for a tag sale that you and your friends or family might hold. Use apostrophes correctly to form contractions and possessives.

Writing Tip

In your writing, remember that a **possessive pronoun** does not include an apostrophe.

This hat is *yours*. (not *your's*)
Which calendar is *hers*?
Its tail is very long.
That boat is *ours*.
Theirs is very old.
Whose keyboard is that?

LESSON 27

THINK ABOUT

Use **quotation marks** at the beginning and end of a **direct quotation**, or the exact words of a speaker. Capitalize the first word of a direct quotation.

Use a **punctuation mark** after the last word of a direct quotation. Use a **comma** when the quotation is a statement or a command and comes *first* in the sentence. Use a **period** when the quotation is a statement or a command and comes *last* in the sentence. Always place a comma or period *before* the quotation mark.

> "The point goes to the Hawks," the referee said.
> The referee said, "The point goes to the Hawks."

- Use a **question mark** or an **exclamation point** after the quotation and before the quotation mark when the quotation itself is a question or an exclamation.

> "Look at that jump!" exclaimed Al.
> Kit responded, "Who is that player?"

- When a direct quotation is **interrupted**, use commas to set off the interrupting *speaker tag*. Begin the second part of the quote with a small letter.

> "Actually," replied Dee, "he's new."

- If a quotation is **more than one sentence**, do not use quotation marks until after the *last* part of the speaker's statement.

> "The penalty is against the Hawks. The home team loses five yards," the referee said.

- A **dialogue** is a conversation that contains direct quotations. When you write dialogue, punctuate it correctly. Start a **new paragraph** each time the speaker changes. Indent each paragraph.

> "This castle must be pretty old," observed Hector as he gazed at the crumbling structure.
> "In fact," Michele replied, "it's several centuries old!"

- Use **quotation marks** before and after the **titles** of *stories, poems, articles,* and *chapters* of books.

> "The Tell-Tale Heart" (story)
> "Fog" (poem)
> "Ten Snowboarding Tips for Teens" (article)
> "Immigration: The Golden Door" (chapter)

- Use **italics** or **underlining** with the **titles** of longer works such as *books, magazines, newspapers, movies, plays,* and *CDs.*

> *The Yearling* (book)   *Patriot Gazette* (newspaper)
> *Teen* (magazine)   *King Kong* (movie)

STUDY A MODEL

Read this passage adapted from the short story "A Retrieved Reformation," by O. Henry.

"Now, Valentine," said the warden, "you'll go out in the morning. Brace up, and make a man of yourself. You're not a bad fellow at heart. Stop cracking safes, and live straight."

"Me?" said Jimmy in surprise. "Why, I never cracked a safe in my life."

"Oh, no," laughed the warden, "of course not. Let's see, now. How was it you happened to get sent up on that Springfield job? It's always one thing or another with you innocent victims."

"Me?" said Jimmy, still virtuous. "Why, warden, I never was in Springfield in my life!"

Quotation marks are red.

 In the first sentence, commas set off the interrupting speaker tag, *said the warden*. The second part of the sentence begins with a small letter.

 Notice the new, indented, paragraph. This signals a new speaker in the dialogue.

 A question mark follows the direct quotation *Me* and precedes the quotation mark because the direct quotation is itself a question.

PRACTICE

A *Write each title correctly. Use quotation marks, or use underlining for italics.*

1. The Medicine Bag (story)
2. Casey at the Bat (poem)
3. America's Heritage (book)
4. Hot News from the Ring of Fire (article)
5. Casablanca (movie)
6. The New York Times (newspaper)
7. Wonders of the Sea (chapter)

B *Read each sentence. Rewrite it, correctly punctuating the quotation. If there are no errors, write Correct.*

1. "My favorite author," said Ellen is Mark Twain".
2. Mother asked, "Is your report due tomorrow?
3. "First place, announced the judge, "goes to Roberto!"
4. "This crossword puzzle is hard. I can't figure out one clue," Chris complained.
5. Pat exclaimed, I have playoff tickets!
6. Miles said, "This job is perfect for you." "You can work outdoors."
7. "Please remain seated, the conductor requested, until the doors open".

C *Read the dialogue. Rewrite it, adding quotation marks as needed.*

What did you do in school today, Son? asked Mr. Bass.

Not much, replied Henry.

Oh, Mr. Bass cried, I'm sure you did something!

I did go to gym class, said Henry, but it was nothing special.

Did you play soccer or practice shooting hoops? Mr. Bass inquired.

Smiling, Henry said, No, I just cleared all the hurdles on the track. I actually broke a school record.

Mr. Bass exclaimed, I would say that was very special, Henry! In fact, I'm very proud of your accomplishments.

Use quotation marks to set off **direct quotations** and the **titles** of stories, poems, articles, and chapters of books. Use **italics** or **underlining** for titles of books, magazines, newspapers, movies, plays, and CDs.

WRITE

Write a summary of a favorite story. Include some dialogue between characters. Make sure to use quotation marks correctly.

Writing Tip

Do not use quotation marks to set off **indirect quotations**, which tell what someone said without using exact words.

Direct: "Hush, class!" said the teacher.
Indirect: The teacher told the class to hush.

LESSON 28

THINK ABOUT

A **paragraph** is a group of sentences about a single idea. A paragraph consists of a *topic sentence* and supporting *detail sentences*. When you write a paragraph, remember to **indent** the first word.

- A **topic sentence** states the main idea, or topic, of a paragraph. The topic sentence may appear anywhere in the paragraph, but it is usually most effective at the beginning or at the end.

   Main Idea: Aztecs created an empire

   Through trade and military conquest, the Aztecs created a vast empire. By the 1500s, Aztec rulers governed between 5 and 15 million people in 38 provinces. At its height, the Aztec empire covered a vast area throughout what is now Central Mexico. (topic sentence at the beginning)

   Main Idea: market at Tenochtitlán
   was a center of trade

   About 60,000 people came every day to the market in Tenochtitlán. Farmers sold beans, sage, tomatoes, peppers, squash, and other produce. Craftsmen sold pottery, leather, jewelry, gold, and sculpture. *Because goods came in from all over the Aztec empire, Tenochtitlán became a center of trade.* (topic sentence at end)

- **Detail sentences** must be related to the main idea of a paragraph. They support the topic sentence with facts, examples, or opinions.

   Fact: Aztec rulers governed 38 provinces.

   Example: In the market at Tenochtitlán, farmers sold beans and peppers.

   Opinion: The Aztec empire was the greatest empire of all time.

- Some **detail sentences** include *sensory words*, which appeal to the five senses. *Sensory details* create vivid mental images for readers.

   A spicy aroma and the drone of multitudes hung over the bustling market in Tenochtitlán.

STUDY A MODEL

Read this paragraph about the planet Venus.

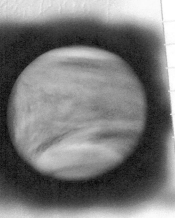

Venus is one of the hottest planets in the solar system. Because Venus is close to the Sun and is surrounded by thick layers of clouds, it absorbs twice as much of the Sun's light as does Earth. Venus undergoes the "greenhouse effect" as carbon dioxide gas in the planet's atmosphere traps heat. As a result, the temperature of Venus averages well over 800°F, which is hot enough to melt lead. Although the surface of Venus features a long channel, this planet has no rivers or oceans. The high temperatures would boil the water away.

The topic sentence is red.

The main idea of this paragraph is that Venus has very high temperatures. The topic sentence, *Venus is one of the hottest planets in the solar system,* presents the main idea.

The detail sentences in this paragraph all develop the main idea, giving specific facts and examples about the high temperatures of Venus.

The final sentence presents an impressive fact about the temperature of Venus.

PRACTICE

A *Read each detail sentence. Write Fact, Example, Opinion, or Sensory Words to tell the primary type of detail used.*

1. A Russian cosmonaut, Yuri Gagarin, was the first human being to orbit Earth.
2. Cereal grains such as wheat and barley were used in ancient Greece.
3. Seatbelts should be worn by everyone.
4. The Uffizi Gallery has the most beautiful artwork in the world.
5. According to the survey, only 20 percent of the citizens support the proposal.
6. The cloaks of Aztec nobles were radiant with brilliant, bold colors.
7. Mars has unusual features, including a volcanic mountain and a vast canyon.

B *Match each detail with the main idea that it develops.*

Main Ideas
1. Arabian horses have an interesting history.
2. Arabian horses are relatively small.
3. Arabian horses have great stamina.

Detail Sentences
a. Most Arabian horses stand five feet from the ground to the high point of the shoulders.
b. Arabian horses excel in endurance races held on long, rough trails.
c. Arabians were bred as desert war horses in the Middle East.

C *Read the paragraph. Rewrite it, deleting the 2 detail sentences that do not develop the main idea. Underline the topic sentence.*

Skyscrapers can have a negative impact on urban areas. Because many commuters work in skyscrapers, the added number of people coming into a city strains sanitation and public transportation systems and increases air pollution from automobiles. In addition, skyscrapers use and waste a large amount of electricity. The first skyscraper was built in Chicago in 1884. If there are high winds or extreme temperature changes, pedestrians may be endangered by falling window glass or sheets of ice. Skyscrapers provide office space, which is needed in overdeveloped cities. Sometimes skyscrapers obstruct air traffic and block bird flyways.

A **paragraph** is a group of sentences about one main idea. The **topic sentence** of a paragraph states the main idea, and **detail sentences** develop it.

WRITE

Research and write a paragraph about a specific planet or about another feature of the solar system. Write a clear topic sentence that states the main idea. Include facts and examples to develop the main idea. Use sensory details if they are appropriate.

Writing Tip

In some kinds of writing, especially expository essays or persuasive essays, some **reasons** that are used as details may be based more on personal experience or preference than on fact.

The president that I admire most is Teddy Roosevelt because he fought to protect and preserve the natural world.

THINK ABOUT

Writing a paragraph with a strong **lead** and effective **transitions** will help you capture and hold the interest of your readers.

- A **lead** is one or two sentences that lead into the rest of a paragraph. Your lead might be an intriguing *question*, a vivid *description*, a thought-provoking *quotation*, or a startling *fact*.

Question:	Do you know the difference between a beaver and a muskrat?
Description:	At the snowy summit, the exhausted explorers proudly planted a flag.
Quotation:	"Please send blankets and dry food," pleaded Mike Foster, director of the shelter.
Fact:	News of Washington's death in 1799 took two weeks to reach Salem, Massachusetts. Today's technology dramatically increases the speed of communication.

- To help ideas flow smoothly in paragraphs, use **transitional words** or phrases that connect ideas by indicating or clarifying different kinds of relationships.

Relationships Shown by Some Transitional Words and Phrases

location: above, among, behind, below, beneath, between, in the distance, in the middle, near, next over, to, toward

time: after, as soon as, before, during, finally, first, last, meanwhile, next, since, soon, then

example: for example, for instance, such as, in addition, furthermore, generally, specifically

emphasis: in fact, indeed, most importantly, nevertheless, regardless

similarities: also, as, both, in the same way, just as, like, likewise, similarly

differences: but, consequently, different from, however, in contrast, on the other hand, unlike, yet

cause/effect: as a result, because, consequently, due to, therefore, thus, so

STUDY A MODEL

Read this paragraph about an invention.

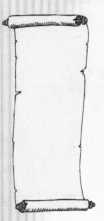

Each person in the United States today uses over 675 pounds of paper per year. People didn't always have paper, however. Before paper, people wrote on surfaces such as stone, metal, cloth, wood, clay, bark, and even tree leaves. Then in A.D. 105, a Chinese official who was in charge of writing court documents searched for a better writing surface. He came up with paper, made from bamboo and mulberry. As a result of this invention, the official's job got easier. Also, paper became available to many people.

The lead is red, and transitional words and phrases are blue.

The lead, a startling fact, grabs readers' interest and leads into the rest of the paragraph.

Always and *Before* are transitional words related to time; *such as* signals examples.

Then indicates time.

As a result signals a cause/effect relationship.

The transitional word *Also* tells that a comparison is being made.

PRACTICE

A *Match each lead sentence with the letter of the word or phrase that best identifies it.*

A question   **B** description   **C** quotation   **D** fact or statistic

1. How many times a day do you use something made of plastic?
2. In *Death of a Salesman*, Willie Loman says, "There's a great future in plastics."
3. Our community recycles 10 tons of plastic every year.
4. A spokesman stated, "Our plant strictly adheres to industry standards."
5. Do you know what indispensable product John Wesley Hyatt invented?
6. The avalanche thundered down the mountain like an express train on a rampage.

B *Read each sentence. Write the transitional word or phrase.*

1. In the same way, the passenger pigeon became extinct.
2. On the other hand, some manufacturers refuse to comply with the law.
3. Most importantly, the number of fatalities declined by 8 percent.
4. As soon as Dr. Desai concluded his speech, most people left.
5. Farming is impossible because almost no rain falls there.
6. After the flood, residents of Baylor sought shelter.
7. For example, European explorers arrived in the 18th century.

C *Read the paragraph. Rewrite it, using appropriate transitional words. Underline the lead sentence.*

What comes in a box in thousands of pieces? Jigsaw puzzles were invented in 1767 by an English mapmaker and engraver, John Spilsbury. Spilsbury wanted to help English children learn about different countries of the world. He turned geography into a game. He mounted a handcolored map on a thin, flat piece of wood. He cut the wood along boundary lines with a fine saw. Students assembled the pieces of the puzzle. Spilsbury's invention helped them learn geography. Puzzles became a form of entertainment.

A **lead** is one or two sentences that lead into the rest of a paragraph. **Transitional words or phrases** help to link ideas within a paragraph.

WRITE

Write a paragraph about a real or imaginary invention or discovery. Write a strong lead and use transitional words and phrases to connect ideas within your paragraph.

Writing Tip

End a paragraph with a **concluding sentence**. A concluding sentence may restate the topic sentence with different words, ask a question, call for an action, state an opinion, or offer a logical conclusion.

Here is another appropriate concluding sentence for the paragraph on page 60 about the invention of paper:

Also, more information eventually became available to more people.

PROOFREADING

Proofreading is the process of finding and correcting errors in written work. Use **proofreading symbols** to note the changes that you want to make in your writing.

Proofreading Symbols	Meanings	Examples
≡	Change a small letter to a capital letter.	capitalize the first letter.
/	Change a capital letter to a small letter.	Make a Small Letter.
¶	Begin a new paragraph.	¶ Start a new paragraph when the main idea changes.
ℒ	Delete this letter, word, punctuation mark, or sentence.	Take out any extra letteres, words words, punctuation marks,, or sentences.
∧	Add a missing letter or word.	Put in missing words or leters.
⌃	Add a comma.	Place a comma here please Sue.
⌄	Add an apostrophe.	This charts examples show how to use proofreaders marks.
⸢⸤ ⸣⸥	Add quotation marks.	Ms. Carr said, Please begin.
⊙	Add a period.	This is the end⊙
?	Add a question mark.	What is your name?
∼ tr	Switch the order of letters or words.	Please your read work carefully.

Here's how one student proofread her draft of an article for the school newsletter.

In my opinion our basketball school teams name should be changed. Our sport's Program should not be identified with a name that offends many people just because it has been in use for decades Many school teams as well as professional teams have successfully changed names without any negative impact. Coach greene is opposed to the name change. He said, My guys like the name. Why fix it if it isnt broken. I disagree because our team should have a name that we can all be proud of whether we Wins or lose.

Proofread the following passage to find the 17 errors. Use proofreading symbols to show how to correct these errors.

From where did the lawn mower come. An textile worker in england invented the first lawn mower in 1830. The worker, Edwin Budding, made some changes to a cutting machine that was used in cloth production. Buddings invention cut dry grass buy means of a roller with cutters special. Advertisements boasted, "Country Gentlemen will find in using my machine an amusing, useful, and healthful exercise. Budding's hand-pushed Mower became popular when it's cost dropped with average citizens. In 1919, Edwin George, an American colonel invented the first gasoline-powered lawn mower. He attached the gas motor, from his wifes washing machine to a hand-pushed mower. Not surprisingly middle-class families soon begin buying powered mowers to mow their lawns.

Rewrite the passage about the lawn mower, making the changes you marked.

PREPARE FOR A TEST

Part I

SELECTION 1

Read this article about urban composting. Then answer questions 1–18.

Turning Trash into Treasure

(1) Local gardener Wes Lind says, "Why not recycle garbage into something useful? (2) Composting is the process what turns waste into rich soil. (3) Anyone are able to compost. (4) Even people in a city composts on a rooftop, patio, or balcony. (5) To compost, gardeners only needs a plastic, metal, or wood compost bin with a lid. (6) Generally, you should have a space that is approximately three feet wide and three feet deep.

(7) First fill the compost bin with a base layer. (8) For the base, use "brown" materials such as sawdust, straw, dry leaves, twigs, and wood chips. (9) Next, make another layer of "green" materials add vegetable parings, egg shells, coffee grounds, weeds, and grass cuttings. (10) Continue to alternate layers of materials. (11) Until the pile is two feet high. (12) Finally, make an indentation in the center of the pile to catch rain.

(13) A compost bin require little maintenance. (14) Occasionally, add scraps to the top of the pile, and making sure the pile is moist. (15) Water, heat, and oxygen help decomposishun. (16) If you turn the pile fairly often, materials will compost more faster. (17) Eventually, you recycled trash into real good soil. (18) You can use this soil yourselves to plant flowers in a windowbox, to cultivate herbs on a windowsill, or growing tomatoes in plastic tubs. (19) You can also donate the soil to residents gardens.

1. What change would correct sentence 1?
   - Ⓐ Add quotation marks before the question mark.
   - Ⓑ Add quotation marks after the question mark.
   - Ⓒ Take out the quotation marks after *says*.
   - Ⓓ Change the capital *W* in *Why* to a small *w*.

2. What change should be made in sentence 2?
   - Ⓐ Change *what* to *that*.
   - Ⓑ Change *what* to *whom*.
   - Ⓒ Change *rich* to *richly*.
   - Ⓓ Change *is* to *are*.

3. The verb in sentence 3 should be changed to
   - Ⓐ *be*.
   - Ⓑ *were*.
   - Ⓒ *have been*.
   - Ⓓ *is*.

4. The verb in sentence 4 should be changed to
   - Ⓐ *composting*.
   - Ⓑ *has composted*.
   - Ⓒ *compost*.
   - Ⓓ *was composting*.

5. What change should be made in sentence 5?
   - Ⓐ Change *needs* to *needing*.
   - Ⓑ Change *needs* to *need*.
   - Ⓒ Place *only* before *you*.
   - Ⓓ Place *with a lid* after *you*.

6. What punctuation change should be made in sentence 7?
   - Ⓐ Add a period after *bin*.
   - Ⓑ Add a question mark after *layer*.
   - Ⓒ Add quotation marks before *First*.
   - Ⓓ Add a comma after *First*.

7. What is the best way to rewrite sentence 9?
   Ⓐ Next, make another layer of "green" materials, add vegetable parings, egg shells, coffee grounds, weeds, and grass cuttings.
   Ⓑ Next, make another layer of "green" materials. Add vegetable parings, egg shells, coffee grounds, weeds, and grass cuttings.
   Ⓒ Next, make another layer of "green" materials add vegetable parings, egg shells, coffee grounds, weeds. And grass cuttings.
   Ⓓ Next, make another layer of "green" materials and add vegetable parings and egg shells and also add coffee grounds, and weeds, or add grass cuttings.

8. What change should be made in sentence 11?
   Ⓐ Change *Until* to *When*.
   Ⓑ Take out the words *two feet*.
   Ⓒ Join the fragment to the end of sentence 10.
   Ⓓ Add a comma after *pile* and join the fragment to the end of sentence 10.

9. What change, if any, should be made in sentence 12?
   Ⓐ Add a coma after *indentation*.
   Ⓑ Make no change.
   Ⓒ Delete the comma after *Finally*.
   Ⓓ Delete the entire sentence.

10. The verb in sentence 13 should be changed to
    Ⓐ *requires*.
    Ⓑ *requiring*.
    Ⓒ *have required*.
    Ⓓ *required*.

11. What change, if any, should be made in sentence 14?
    Ⓐ Delete the comma before *and*.
    Ⓑ Change *making* to *make*.
    Ⓒ Change *moist* to *moister*.
    Ⓓ Make no change.

12. What word change should be made in sentence 15?
    Ⓐ Change *decomposishun* to *decomposition*.
    Ⓑ Change *decomposishun* to *composishun*.
    Ⓒ Change *oxygen* to *air*.
    Ⓓ Change *water* to *steam*.

13. In sentence 16, *more faster* should be changed to
    Ⓐ *most faster.*
    Ⓑ *more fasterer.*
    Ⓒ *faster.*
    Ⓓ *fastest.*

14. Which verb should replace *recycled* in sentence 17?
    Ⓐ *recycling.*
    Ⓑ *will have recycled.*
    Ⓒ *had recycled.*
    Ⓓ *were recycled.*

15. In sentence 17, what change should be made?
    Ⓐ Change *good* to *well.*
    Ⓑ Change *good* to *bad.*
    Ⓒ Change *real* to *really.*
    Ⓓ Change *real* to *sure.*

16. In sentence 18, *yourselves* should be changed to
    Ⓐ *themselves.*
    Ⓑ *herself.*
    Ⓒ *myself.*
    Ⓓ *yourself.*

17. Which change should be made in sentence 18?
    Ⓐ Change *growing* to *to grow.*
    Ⓑ Change *to plant* to *planted.*
    Ⓒ Change *to cultivate* to *were cultivating.*
    Ⓓ Change *on a windowsill* to *in a windowsill.*

18. What change should be made in sentence 19?
    Ⓐ Add a comma after *donate.*
    Ⓑ Add a question mark after *garden.*
    Ⓒ Insert an apostrophe after the *s* in *residents.*
    Ⓓ Insert quotation marks at the beginning.

Read this essay about the Galápagos Islands. Then answer questions 19–36.

The Galápagos Islands

(1) Why are the Galápagos Islands so fascinating? (2) These islands are some of the most unusualest islands on the earth. (3) Located in the Pacific Ocean, the Galápagos lie 600 miles west of ecuador in South America. (4) The Galápagos spread out over 3,000 miles. (5) The Galápagos consist of more than 20 individual islands. (6) Most of these islands is shield volcanoes, covered with layers of hardened lava.

(7) The first recorded discovery of the galápagos islands was in 1535. (8) In 1570, a mapmaker named they *Isolas de Galápagos*, or Islands of the Tortoises. (9) During the 1600s, British pirates, whom looted Spanish Ships, used the islands as a hideout. (10) Charles Darwin, a British scientist, sailed to the islands on the *beagle* in 1835.

(11) By the end of his stay, Darwin have discovered some very unique animals. (12) Among the island most rarest birds are 13 species of finches, flightless cormorants, and Galápagos penguins. (13) The only sea lizard in the world is the marine iguana. (14) The marine iguana can be found in the islands. (15) The Galápagos are also home to giant tortoises that weigh more than 500 pounds and can live for 150 years!

(16) In the Galápagos Islands Darwin also discovered distinctive plants. (17) Some of these plants includes a salt-resistant tomato, distinct species of cotton and pepper, and the prickly pear cactus that grows on lava rocks. (18) The daisy tree is the rarest plant in view of the fact that it is found only on Santiago Island. (19) Today, scientists still study the variety of wildlife of the Galápagos. (20) Tourists still study the variety of wildlife of the Galápagos.

19. Sentence 1, the lead sentence of this paragraph, captures readers' interest with a
    Ⓐ question.
    Ⓑ description.
    Ⓒ quotation.
    Ⓓ fact.

20. In sentence 2, *most unusualest* should be changed to
    Ⓐ *unusualest.*
    Ⓑ *more unusualest.*
    Ⓒ *most unusual.*
    Ⓓ *unusual.*

21. What change in capitalization should be made in sentence 3?
    Ⓐ Change *Pacific Ocean* to *Pacific ocean.*
    Ⓑ Change *west* to *West.*
    Ⓒ Change *ecuador* to *Ecuador.*
    Ⓓ Change *South America* to *south America.*

22. To provide variety, which is the best combination of sentences 4 and 5?
    Ⓐ The Galápagos spread out over 3,000 miles, and the Galápagos consist of more than 20 individual islands.
    Ⓑ The Galápagos, which consist of more than 20 individual islands, spread out over 3,000 miles.
    Ⓒ The Galápagos spread out over 3,000 miles the Galápagos consist of more than 20 individual islands.
    Ⓓ The Galápagos spread out over 3,000 miles; the Galápagos consist of more than 20 individual islands.

23. What change should be made in sentence 6?
    Ⓐ Change *is* to *are.*
    Ⓑ Change *is* to *being.*
    Ⓒ Change *covered* to *covering.*
    Ⓓ Insert a comma after *hardened.*

24. In sentence 7, what change should be made?
    Ⓐ Change *was* to *were.*
    Ⓑ Insert a comma between *first* and *recorded.*
    Ⓒ Change *galápagos islands* to *Galápagos islands.*
    Ⓓ Change *galápagos islands* to *Galápagos Islands.*

25. In sentence 8, the pronoun *they* should be changed to
    Ⓐ *them.*
    Ⓑ *we.*
    Ⓒ *it.*
    Ⓓ *their.*

26. Which capitalization change should be made in sentence 9?
    Ⓐ Change *Spanish* to *spanish.*
    Ⓑ Change *islands* to *Islands.*
    Ⓒ Change *Ships* to *ships.*
    Ⓓ Change *hideout* to *Hideout.*

27. In sentence 9, the pronoun *whom* should be changed to
    Ⓐ *that.*
    Ⓑ *which.*
    Ⓒ *whose.*
    Ⓓ *who.*

28. What change would correct sentence 10?
    Ⓐ Change *Charles Darwin* to *charles darwin.*
    Ⓑ Change *British* to *british.*
    Ⓒ Change *scientist* to *Scientist.*
    Ⓓ Change *beagle* to *Beagle.*

29. In sentence 11, the helping verb *have* should be changed to
    Ⓐ *will have.*
    Ⓑ *has.*
    Ⓒ *had.*
    Ⓓ *having.*

30. In sentence 12, what change should be made to the word *island*?
    Ⓐ Add an apostrophe and an *s* to *island.*
    Ⓑ Add an *s* and an apostrophe to *island.*
    Ⓒ Add an *s* to *island.*
    Ⓓ Add *es* to *island.*

31. In sentence 12, which change should be made?
    - Ⓐ Change *are* to *is*.
    - Ⓑ Change *most rarest* to *more* rarest.
    - Ⓒ Change *most rarest* to *rarest*.
    - Ⓓ Change *finches* to *Finches*.

32. What is the best way to join sentences 13 and 14?
    - Ⓐ The only sea lizard in the world is the marine iguana and the marine iguana can be found in the islands.
    - Ⓑ The marine iguana, the only sea lizard in the world, can be found in the islands.
    - Ⓒ The only sea lizard in the world can be found in the islands, the marine iguana.
    - Ⓓ Because the only sea lizard in the world is the marine iguana, the marine iguana can be found in the islands.

33. What change, if any, should be made to sentence 16?
    - Ⓐ Change *Darwin* to *Darwin's*.
    - Ⓑ Change *discovered* to *has discovered*.
    - Ⓒ Make no change.
    - Ⓓ Insert a comma after *Islands*.

34. What change should be made in sentence 17?
    - Ⓐ Change *these* to *them*.
    - Ⓑ Change *includes* to *include*.
    - Ⓒ Insert a comma between *prickly* and *pear*.
    - Ⓓ Change *that* to *what*.

35. What change should be made in sentence 18 to eliminate unnecessary words?
    - Ⓐ Change *in view of the fact that* to *because*.
    - Ⓑ Delete *that*.
    - Ⓒ Delete *is*.
    - Ⓓ Change *Santiago Island* to *one island*.

36. What is the best way to join sentences 19 and 20?
    - Ⓐ Today, scientists still study the variety of wildlife of the Galápagos, and tourists still study the variety of wildlife of the Galápagos also.
    - Ⓑ Today, scientists and tourists still study the variety of wildlife of the Galápagos.
    - Ⓒ Today, scientists still study the variety of wildlife of the Galápagos tourists still study the variety of wildlife of the Galápagos.
    - Ⓓ Today, scientists still study the variety of wildlife of the Galápagos because tourists still study the variety of wildlife of the Galápagos.

Read this biographical sketch of American artist George Catlin. Then answer questions 37–54.

George Catlin (1796–1872)

(1) As a young man, George Catlin pursued a career in law. (2) While trying cases, he often doodled caricatures on the lawyers table. (3) After moving to Philadelphia, Catlin lost interest in his law practice. (4) Instead, him became an artist.

(5) Catlin was self-taught. (6) He earned a living by painting miniature portraits. (7) When he had achieved success, he took up another challenge. (8) He decided to paint native americans, so he took his first trip to the West in 1830. (9) Catlin rode on horseback, took a steamboat, and paddled a canoe carrying his supplies. (10) Explorer William Clark offered he help. (11) Clark was an important leader. (12) Clark had conducted an expedition to the West in 1804.

(13) Over a period of 7 years, Catlin painted portraits of Native Americans. (14) In 48 different tribes. (15) The Seminole inhabited Florida. (16) Catlin carefully observed and recorded images of Native Americans and there traditional dances, religious ceremonies, and hunting parties. (17) During his quest to capture Native American life, Catlin painted mens, womens, and childrens portraits. (18) Catlin's artwork reflected his interest in Native American cultures.

(19) Eventually, Catlin launched an ambitious traveling exhibit of Native American paintings, sketches, costumes, drums, bows, and other artifact's. (20) He showed Catlin's Indian Gallery to eager americans and europeans. (21) Several times Catlin had offered to sell his exhibit to the United States government but the government always refused to buy it so Catlin's collection remained in a dirty basement for more than 30 years. (22) After Catlin's death, his collection was donated to the smithsonian institution in 1879.

37. What change should be made in sentence 2?
    Ⓐ   Place *While trying cases* before *on*.
    Ⓑ   Place *often* after *table*.
    Ⓒ   Change *doodled* to *drew*.
    Ⓓ   Change *lawyers* to *lawyer's*.

38. Which word in sentence 3 is an abstract noun?
    Ⓐ   *interest*
    Ⓑ   *Catlin*
    Ⓒ   *lost*
    Ⓓ   *Philadelphia*

39. In sentence 4, the object pronoun *him* should be changed to
    Ⓐ   the object pronoun *them*.
    Ⓑ   the object pronoun *it*.
    Ⓒ   the subject pronoun *they*.
    Ⓓ   the subject pronoun *he*.

40. To create a complex sentence, how should sentences 5 and 6 be changed?
    Ⓐ   Catlin was self-taught, and he earned a living painting miniature portraits.
    Ⓑ   Although Catlin was self-taught, he earned a living painting miniature portraits.
    Ⓒ   Catlin was self-taught; he earned a living painting miniature portraits.
    Ⓓ   Catlin was self-taught, but he earned a living painting miniature portraits.

41. What change, if any, should be made in sentence 7?
    Ⓐ   Add a comma after *When*.
    Ⓑ   Delete the comma after *success*.
    Ⓒ   Add a comma after *another*.
    Ⓓ   Make no change.

42. What change should be made in sentence 8?
    Ⓐ   Change *West* to *west*.
    Ⓑ   Change *trip* to *Trip*.
    Ⓒ   Change *native americans* to *native Americans*.
    Ⓓ   Change *native americans* to *Native Americans*.

43. How would sentence 9 look if it were written correctly?
   Ⓐ Catlin rode on horseback, taking a steamboat, and paddled a canoe carrying his supplies.
   Ⓑ Carrying his supplies, Catlin rode on horseback, took a steamboat, and paddled a canoe.
   Ⓒ Catlin rode on horseback, took a steamboat, and he paddled a canoe carrying his supplies.
   Ⓓ Catlin rode on horseback, took a steamboat, and paddled a canoe. Carrying his supplies.

44. In sentence 10, what change should be made?
   Ⓐ Insert a comma after *Clark*.
   Ⓑ Change *William Clark* to *william clark*.
   Ⓒ Change *he* to *him*.
   Ⓓ Change *he* to *they*.

45. What is the best way to join sentences 11 and 12?
   Ⓐ Clark was an important leader, he had conducted an expedition to the West in 1804.
   Ⓑ Clark was an important leader but Clark had conducted an expedition to the West in 1804.
   Ⓒ Clark, an important leader, had conducted an expedition to the West in 1804.
   Ⓓ Clark was an important leader Clark had conducted an expedition to the West in 1804.

46. Which is the best combination of sentences 13 and 14?
   Ⓐ Over a period of 7 years, Catlin painted portraits of Native Americans, and in 48 different tribes.
   Ⓑ Over a period of 7 years, Catlin painted portraits of Native Americans; in 48 different tribes.
   Ⓒ In 48 tribes, Catlin painted portraits of Native Americans over a period of 7 years.
   Ⓓ Over a period of 7 years, Catlin painted portraits of Native Americans in 48 different tribes.

47. Sentence 15 does not belong in the paragraph because
   Ⓐ it contains incorrect information.
   Ⓑ it is a sentence fragment.
   Ⓒ it does not support the main idea of the paragraph.
   Ⓓ it is a rambling sentence.

48. In sentence 16, what change should be made?
   Ⓐ Change *there* to *their*.
   Ⓑ Change *there* to *they're*.
   Ⓒ Place *carefully* after *images*.
   Ⓓ Change *recorded* to *will have recorded*.

49. The possessive nouns in sentence 17 should be written
    Ⓐ *men's, women's, and childrens'.*
    Ⓑ *mens, women's, and children's.*
    Ⓒ *men's, women's, and children's.*
    Ⓓ *mens', womens', and childrens'.*

50. In the third paragraph, the topic sentence is
    Ⓐ sentence 15.
    Ⓑ sentence 16.
    Ⓒ sentence 17.
    Ⓓ sentence 18.

51. Which change should be made to sentence 19?
    Ⓐ Change the capital letters in *Native Americans* to small letters.
    Ⓑ Delete the apostrophe in *artifact's.*
    Ⓒ Add a question mark as end punctuation.
    Ⓓ Switch the order of *traveling* and *exhibit.*

52. What change should be made in sentence 20?
    Ⓐ Change *he* to *him.*
    Ⓑ Change *americans and europeans* to *Americans and Europeans.*
    Ⓒ Change *Catlin's Indian Gallery* to *Catlin's indian gallery.*
    Ⓓ Change *showed* to *showing.*

53. Which is the best revision of sentence 21?
    Ⓐ Several times Catlin had offered to sell his exhibit to the United States government, but the government always refused to buy it. As a result, Catlin's collection remained in a dirty basement for more than 30 years.
    Ⓑ Several times Catlin had offered to sell his exhibit to the United States government but the government always refused to buy it, so Catlin's collection remained in a dirty basement for more than 30 years.
    Ⓒ Several times Catlin had offered to sell his exhibit to the United States government. The government always refused to buy it. Catlin's collection remained in a dirty basement for more than 30 years.
    Ⓓ Several times Catlin had offered to sell his exhibit to the United States government, the government always refused to buy it Catlin's collection remained in a dirty basement for more than 30 years.

54. Which change should be made in sentence 22?
    Ⓐ Change *smithsonian institution* to *"smithsonian institution."*
    Ⓑ Change *smithsonian institution* to *Smithsonian Institution.*
    Ⓒ Change *was donated* to *were donated.*
    Ⓓ Change *was donated* to *donated.*

PART II In Lessons 31–37 you write. Use what you've learned in Part I to *WRITE!*

LESSON 31

DESCRIPTIVE ESSAYS

A **description** creates mental pictures in readers' minds. When you write a **descriptive essay**, you carefully chose words to create vivid images of specific people, places, or things. To do this, you can use **comparisons** and **sensory language** (words that appeal to the sense of sight, sound, taste, smell, or touch).

Here is a sample writing prompt for a descriptive essay.

> *Write an essay describing a person you know well.*

Read this descriptive essay, which was written in response to the prompt. Then read the Writing Tips to learn more about descriptive essays.

Writing Tips

❖ Before writing a description of a person, ask yourself questions about the person's
  • appearance.
  • facial expressions.
  • behavior.
  • personality traits.

  Jot down whatever comes to mind.

❖ Give your descriptive essay an interesting title and a clear beginning, middle, and ending. Introduce your subject at the beginning.

❖ Use a logical pattern of organization. When describing a person, you might use order of impression, based on your emotional response to your subject.

❖ Show instead of tell. When describing a person, use actions and dialogue as part of the description.

❖ Whenever possible, choose precise words to capture your subject. Use specific nouns, strong verbs, and vivid adjectives and adverbs. Think of your 5 senses, and use sensory language when appropriate.

❖ If possible, use comparisons such as similes ("He is as tall as a skyscraper") or metaphors ("He is a towering skyscraper") to paint vivid pictures with words.

Nana

Once when I was young, I visited my great-grandmother at her cottage on the Maine coast. Nana drank fragrant peppermint tea, and I munched on juicy fig bars that she had baked herself. While I sat quietly on a scratchy armchair, Nana told me fascinating stories about her life. She grew up in a hotel that her parents owned in Plainfield, New Jersey. Sometimes she pretended that she was one of the guests. My favorite story was how she bought her cottage from a fisherman and had workers roll the cottage on logs right up to where it is now, next to the beach.

When she was a young woman, Nana traveled around the world. She has a large glass cabinet crowded with gold coins, carved jade, and stone sculptures. "This one came from a bazaar in China," Nana said. "I nearly lost it on the steamship home."

Nana also told me that she had played in a local symphony orchestra. "Nana, would you play for me?" I asked.

Glancing at me with twinkling blue eyes, Nana picked up her violin and tucked it under her chin. The smooth body of the violin rested on her slight shoulder. Then Nana grasped the bow with her thin hand, as white as snow. She moved the bow back and forth across the strings. Slow, sad violin music filled the air. As she played, Nana swayed slightly to the rhythm. I felt honored that Nana performed a solo for one of her biggest fans—me!

USING GRAPHIC ORGANIZERS

Before you write, use graphic organizers to help yourself think about, gather, and sort information for your descriptive essay.

The writer of the descriptive essay about Nana on page 76 might have used a Sensory Words Chart, such as the one below.

Sight	twinkling blue eyes, hand as white as snow, slight shoulder
Sound	sad violin music
Taste	peppermint tea, juicy fig bars
Touch	scratchy armchair, smooth body of the violin
Smell	peppermint tea

A Sensory Words Chart helps writers gather and organize information related to some or all of the five senses. These sensory details can then be used to create vivid images.

The writer of the descriptive essay on page 76 might also have used a Descriptive Details Cluster such as the one below. If you had been the writer, what descriptive details would you have used to create strong images of Nana? Fill in the ovals with descriptive details that tell how Nana looked, how she acted, etc.

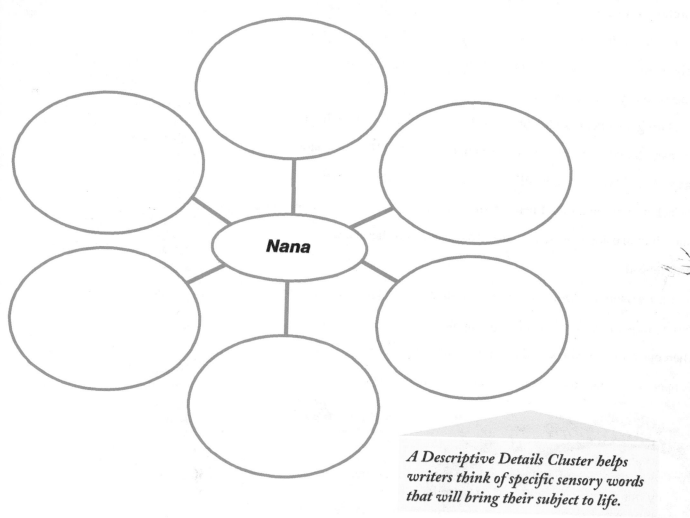

A Descriptive Details Cluster helps writers think of specific sensory words that will bring their subject to life.

TAKING A LOOK AT DESCRIPTIVE ESSAYS

 **Score: 4**

Read the descriptive essay below, which was written in response to the prompt on page 76. This description scored a 4 on a scale that ranges from 1 to 4 (with 4 being the best). Next, read the comments and think about why this description scored a 4.

1

Coach Hopper

My field hockey coach is Louanne Hopper. During practice, Coach Hopper sprints up and down the grassy field like a colt. If someone makes a mistake, she blows her whistle shrilly. If one of us makes a good save or passes well, she yells, That's fine, okay now, you've got it!"

Before a big game, Coach Hopper makes sure we wear spotless uniforms and tie our hair back neatly. She herself wears a womens suit as if she's going to a business meeting. Quietly, she asks us to sit down in a circle, and then she allows each of us to say something or to ask questions. As she goes over last-minute pointers, she twirls her short curly hair nervously. Usually she ends by telling us, "The most important thing is to play with pride."

During a game, Coach Hopper is like a cheerleader who whoops for our team. Standing in front of the bench, she shouts, "Hey, nice stop, Nastasi!" or "Way to go, Hall!" When a game is tied, she fidgets with her jacket or crouches on a bended knee. If a penalty is called against our team, the Lakeside Otters, then she groans and slaps her hand against her forehead.

Last season, the Otters went to the regional championships. As the starters took the field, Coach Hopper applauded wildly. She beamed when our rookie goalie saved a point. Although we didn't win, Coach Hopper still treated us like champions. She's a great coach!

2

PARTNER COMMENTS

Your details and dialogue helped me picture Coach Hopper in my mind. I wish I could have a coach like her!

3

Your Turn

Now it's your turn to help the writer. Find and fix the errors in the writing. Go back to the pages in green if you need help.

1. Find and fix the missing **quotation marks**. See pp. 56–57.

2. Find and fix the incorrect **possessive noun**. See pp. 8–9.

TEACHER COMMENTS

4

▲ Your title tells me right away who you're describing. Good!

▲ Descriptive details and dialogue help me form a clear mental image of Coach Hopper.

▲ Your comparisons really help me "see" the coach. The comparison of Coach Hopper to a colt shows me that she is young, athletic, and energetic.

▲ Precise words like *pointers, whoops, fidgets,* and *beamed* make your description come alive.

▲ You've done a good job of varying sentence structure and varying the types of sentences you use.

▲ Your essay's organization (at practice, before a game, and during a game) works well.

▲ Your conclusion sums it up.

Read the descriptive essay and the comments that follow. Think about why this description scored a 3.

1

A Great Coach

I know Louanne Hopper well. I play on the field hockey team, and she is my coach. She is not too strict, but she make us practice a lot. I go to practice nearly every day after school.

Coach Hopper is not very tall, but she can run fast like a racehorse. She runs up and down the field during our practices. She yells encouragement when she sees something good. She blows her whistle when she sees something bad. That whistle sounds like a screeching bird!

Before an important game, Coach Hopper makes sure that all the girls look neat and clean. She lets us talk about the game and anything else that might be bothering us. Then she give us a pep talk. She really wants our team, the Lakeside otters, to perform well.

During a game, our coach screams more louder than anyone else. If the game is tied, she gets real nervous and can't sit still. Coach Hopper gets very upset if a referee calls a penalty against our team which happens sometimes.

When our team went to the state championships, Coach Hopper was on pins and needles. We didn't win, but Coach Hopper told us we were still winners.

2

PARTNER COMMENTS

More details and sensory words would have made the coach seem more real. It was a good description though.

3

Your Turn

Now it's your turn to help the writer. Find and fix the errors in the writing. Go back to the pages in green if you need help.

1. Find and fix the two errors in **subject-verb agreement**. See pp. 18–19.
2. Find and fix the **capitalization** error. See pp. 50–51.
3. Find and fix the **double comparison**. See pp. 24–25.
4. Find and fix the **adjective** that should be an **adverb**. See pp. 26–27.
5. Find and fix the **dependent clause** that is missing a **comma**. See pp. 12–13, 30–31, 36–37, and 52–53.

TEACHER COMMENTS

4

▲ Nice job introducing the subject in your title and opening paragraph.

▲ Your ideas are arranged in a logical sequence. Good.

▲ The comparison of your coach to a racehorse and her whistle to a screeching bird help me picture her.

▲ You use some variety with sentences, but you should try **combining** some short **sentences** into longer ones. See pp. 30–31, 34–39, and 44–45 for help.

▲ "Show" more than "tell." Try using even more **sensory details** to describe how Coach Hopper looks, talks, and acts. See pp. 58–59.

▲ Your ending is good, but you could add something about how the coach's attitude made the team feel.

Score: 2

Read the descriptive essay and the comments that follow. Think about why this description scored a 2.

1

I play field hockey. My coach is louanne Hopper. She is tough but kind she gives us a lot of tips she wants to help us play field hockey more better.

Coach Hopper call us together before a game. She lets us talk, and she answers questions. Then I'm ready to play. Because I know what to due. Sometimes Coach Hopper is very nervous. She hops up and down. Sometimes she get excited and cheers for us. The best of all is that she thinks you are a winner even if you do not always win.

Coach Hopper is active she runs up and down the field without getting tired. She yells helpful comments when my teammates plays a good game. One day I used my stick to pass the ball to another player. My coach said I played a real good game.

2

PARTNER COMMENTS

I could tell that you were describing your field hockey coach, but you didn't give enough details.

3

Your Turn

Now it's your turn to help the writer. Find and fix the errors in the writing. Go back to the pages in green if you need help.

1. Find and fix the **capitalization** error. See pp. 46–47.
2. Find and fix the two **run-on sentences**. See pp. 40–41.
3. Find and fix the **double comparison**. See pp. 24–25.
4. Find and fix the three errors in **subject-verb agreement**. See pp. 18–19.
5. Find and fix the **sentence fragment**. See pp. 34–35.
6. Find and fix the incorrect **homophone**. See pp. 28–29.
7. Find and fix the **adjective** that should be an **adverb**. See pp. 26–27.

TEACHER COMMENTS

4

▲ Please add an appropriate title to your description.

▲ Use some comparisons to build your description. For example, you could say that the coach "hops up and down like a giant grasshopper."

▲ You could add more **precise words** and **sensory words** to help readers form strong mental pictures. Remember to show rather than tell. See pp. 4–5, 22–27, and 58–59 for help.

▲ Use different kinds of sentences. Many begin with *I* or *she* and are too short. Try **combining** some short **sentences** or **varying** the structure of some **sentences**. See pp. 30-31, 34–39, and 44-45.

▲ Your description doesn't follow a logical order. This makes it confusing for me to read.

▲ To make your description more realistic, turn Coach Hopper's words into **dialogue**. See pp. 56–57.

Score: 1

Read the descriptive essay and the comments that follow. Think about why this description scored a 1.

1

My cousin is very quick and strong. She plays sports. She has a female coach. The players say she is strict but also nice. The coachs experiance is great. Most of the players likes the coach. Some of them feels worried they might make a mistake. The team practice every afternoon on the field. The players work hard. So they can be better players.

The basketball team won a championship last year. They are the woodpeckers. The players theirselfs won there last game. My cousin a forward on the team scored the winning point. The coach itself cheered for the excellent effort the team will go on to more wins.

PARTNER COMMENTS

2

Your essay needs a title. You should have written about your cousin since you know her so well. Why did you mention the basketball team?

TEACHER COMMENTS

3

▲ The essay should describe a person you know well. Please follow the prompt.

▲ Your description lacks specific details. Use **sensory words** that appeal to sight, sound, taste, smell, or touch. See pp. 58–59 for help.

▲ Add some comparisons to strengthen your imagery.

▲ Your essay needs a clearer beginning, middle , and ending.

▲ Dialogue helps create mental pictures of people. Can you turn some sentences into **dialogue**? See pp. 56–57.

▲ Avoid sentences with **details** that do not develop the **main idea**. See pp. 58–59.

4

Your Turn

Now it's your turn to help the writer. Find and fix the errors in the writing. Go back to the pages in green if you need help.

1. Find and fix the incorrect **possessive noun**. See pp. 8–9.

2. Find and fix the misspelled **noun suffix**. See pp. 6–7.

3. Find and fix the three errors in **subject-verb agreement**. See pp. 18–21.

4. Find and fix the **sentence fragment**. See pp. 34–35.

5. Find and fix the **capitalization** error. See pp. 50–51.

6. Find and fix the two incorrect **intensive pronouns**. See pp. 14–15.

7. Find and fix the incorrect **homophone**. See pp. 28–29.

8. Find and fix the **appositive phrase** that should be set off by commas. See pp. 38–39.

9. Find and fix the **run-on sentence**. See pp. 40–41.

USING A RUBRIC TO SCORE DESCRIPTIVE ESSAYS

This rubric is based on a point scale of 1 to 4. It was used to score the descriptive essays on pages 78–81. Use this rubric to remember what is important in descriptive essays.

4 — A score of 4 means that the writer

- ☐ connects the writing directly to the prompt.
- ☐ almost always uses the correct forms of words.
- ☐ almost always uses capitalization and punctuation correctly.
- ☐ almost always uses clear and complete sentences and includes sentence variety.
- ☐ creates a title that clearly relates to the description.
- ☐ introduces the subject clearly at the beginning.
- ☐ creates a clear beginning, middle, and ending.
- ☐ uses interesting details and sensory words to create strong images for readers.
- ☐ uses comparisons, such as similes and metaphors, to strengthen the imagery.
- ☐ uses an effective pattern of organization, such as spatial order or chronological order.
- ☐ begins a new paragraph for each change of idea or speaker.

2 — A score of 2 means that the writer

- ☐ connects the writing to the prompt in a general way.
- ☐ uses some incorrect forms of words.
- ☐ makes some errors in capitalization or punctuation.
- ☐ uses little sentence variety.
- ☐ uses some run-on or rambling sentences or sentence fragments.
- ☐ usually creates a title that relates in some way to the description.
- ☐ presents the subject somewhere within the description.
- ☐ creates a weak beginning, middle, or ending.
- ☐ includes too few interesting details or sensory words to create strong images for readers.
- ☐ uses no comparisons or uses them unsuccessfully.
- ☐ uses a weak pattern of organization.
- ☐ may make some paragraphing errors.

3 — A score of 3 means that the writer

- ☐ connects the writing to the prompt.
- ☐ usually uses the correct forms of words.
- ☐ usually uses capitalization and punctuation correctly.
- ☐ usually uses clear and complete sentences and includes some sentence variety.
- ☐ creates a title that relates to the description.
- ☐ introduces the subject toward the beginning.
- ☐ creates a beginning, middle, and ending.
- ☐ uses some interesting details and sensory words to create images for readers.
- ☐ uses some simple comparisons to strengthen the imagery.
- ☐ uses an appropriate pattern of organization.
- ☐ usually begins a new paragraph for each change of idea or speaker.

1 — A score of 1 means that the writer

- ☐ does not successfully connect the writing to the prompt.
- ☐ uses many incorrect forms of words.
- ☐ makes many errors in capitalization or punctuation.
- ☐ uses almost no sentence variety.
- ☐ uses several run-on or rambling sentences or sentence fragments.
- ☐ usually creates a poor title or has no title at all.
- ☐ identifies the subject in an unclear way or not at all.
- ☐ creates a description without a clear beginning, middle, or ending.
- ☐ uses words and details that fail to create strong images for readers.
- ☐ uses no comparisons.
- ☐ uses no consistent pattern of organization.
- ☐ may make many paragraphing errors.

SCORING DESCRIPTIVE ESSAYS

Now it's your turn to score some descriptive essays. The four descriptive essays on pages 83 and 84 were written in response to this prompt.

Write an essay describing a favorite thing that you own.

Read each descriptive essay. Write a few comments about it. Then give it a score from 1 to 4. Think about what you've learned in this lesson as you match each description with its correct score.

Model A

Score: ▽

I like my jacket on account of the fact that its real old and soft. It is light blue. Like the sky. It has a patch on one sleeve, I fell and tore it one day. I wear this jean jacket all the time. I dont mind that the front pockets of the jacket is frayed. It has two deep side pockets also. You can keep you're money or keys in them. The buttons is metal. Some are very loose and they are hanging off but I can sew them back on with blue thread.

Comments:_____
_____
_____
_____
_____
_____
_____
_____

Model B

Score: ▽

My jean jacket is old, its faded and worn. Many of the buttons is loose. Their not shiny anymore they rusted after I walked in the rain. Sometimes it is to cold, so I put on another jacket that is more warmer. I have a wool jacket. My jackets blue material look awful now. I cant say why I like this jacket but I usually wears it. When the weather is nice.

Comments:_____
_____
_____
_____
_____
_____
_____
_____

SCORING DESCRIPTIVE ESSAYS *continued*

Model C

Score: ▽

My Jeans Jacket

My jeans jacket has frayed cuffs and baggy sleeves. Its round metal buttons are no longer shiny silver. Some of the big blue stitches are loose. The denim is faded and almost bare at the elbows, and one of the two front pockets flap in the breeze. Still, this old jacket is my favorite possession.

One reason I love my jacket is that the fabric is no longer stiff and rough. The denim now feels as soft as cotton balls or kitten's fur. Another reason is that I've added my own touches over the years. My jacket has a small patch on the left elbow and embroidery designs that I sewed on the collar and back.

The main reason I like my jacket so much is that I bought it while I was shopping with a friend. Betsy and I spent hours getting new clothes for school. Later that year, Betsy unexpectedly moved to another town. Whenever I wear my comfortable jacket, I think of Betsy and smile.

*Comments:*_____

_____

_____

_____

_____

_____

_____

_____

Model D

Score: ▽

My Favorite Thing

My dusty faded jean jacket is my favorite thing. I know the denim is thin in spots, but the fabric is soft as silk, or satin. When I put it on it feels light and comfortable. I like the different colors of my jacket, too. In some places, it is blue like the ocean.

Some of the metal buttons are missing and the left front pocket is half torn off. Once I fell and ripped a hole in the elbow, I sewed a patch on it. The cuffs are worn, and the stitches are coming undone. Despite all this I love my jacket. Whenever I wear my jacket, I smile. I think of all the good times I had while I wore it.

*Comments:*_____

_____

_____

_____

_____

_____

_____

WRITING A DESCRIPTIVE ESSAY

Now you get to write your own descriptive essay. Use the prompt below.

> *Write an essay describing someone whom you admire.*

2 (place)

When You Write Your Descriptive Essay

1. **Think about** what you want to write. Close your eyes and think about the person you want to describe. Ask yourself some questions.

   - What does this person look like?
   - What does he or she sound like?
   - What are the person's strongest personality traits?

   Use graphic organizers to gather and sort the information.

2. **Write** your first draft. Your descriptive essay should be four to five paragraphs long and should have a clear beginning, middle, and ending.

3. **Read** your draft. Use the checklist that your teacher will give you to review your writing.

4. **Edit** your description. Make changes until your description creates strong images.

5. **Proofread** your descriptive essay one last time.

6. **Write** a neat copy of your descriptive essay and give it to your partner.

Work with a Partner

7. **Read** your partner's descriptive essay.

8. **Score** your partner's descriptive essay from 1 to 4, using the rubric on page 82. Then complete the Partner Comments sheet that your teacher will give you. Tell what you like about the description and what you think would make it better.

9. **Switch** papers.

10. **Think about** your partner's comments. Read your essay again. Make changes that you think will improve your descriptive essay.

11. **Write** a neat final copy of your descriptive essay.

Making Connections

As you read books and magazines, notice how sensory details are used to create vivid mental images. Look for examples of similes (comparisons using the words *like* or *as*) or metaphors (comparisons that do not use *like* or *as*).

- Think about different ways you could arrange a descriptive essay. For example, you might describe an athlete's physical appearance from top to bottom (spatial order), his or her personality traits from most to least important (order of importance), or his or her actions during important games (chronological order).

- Remember that when you describe people, you can include details about how they behave. Does someone chuckle, scratch their head, scowl, or fidget? Keep notes on people's behavior. You can use the notes to flesh out future descriptions.

85

PERSONAL NARRATIVES

You tell stories all the time. Some are true, and some are invented. Some are about others, and some are about you. A true story that tells about something that has happened in your own life is called a personal narrative. Here is a sample writing prompt for a personal narrative.

> *Write about an accomplishment that made you feel proud.*

Read this personal narrative, which was written in response to the prompt. Then read the Writing Tips to learn more about personal narratives.

Writing Tips

* You can write about anything in your life, from the everyday to the momentous.

* When you write a personal narrative, remember that the story is about you, and you are the narrator. Use the first-person pronouns *I, me, we,* and *us.*

* Arrange your story with a clear beginning, middle, and ending.

* Use transitional words such as *first, next,* or *last* to help your readers follow the order of events and understand the relationships between events.

* Whenever possible, use precise, interesting words and phrases to bring your experience to life. For example, instead of telling readers that the pumpkins were green, tell them that the pumpkins looked like green balloons.

* Include some realistic dialogue among the characters to make your narrative come alive. Remember to use quotation marks and indentation correctly.

* Add a title that will interest readers in your personal narrative. Tell something about the subject of your narrative without giving too much away.

My Green Thumb

Last spring, I planted my first vegetable garden all by myself. First, I drew a picture of my backyard on a sheet of paper. In one corner, I made a big square and sketched in rows. Then I wrote down the kinds of vegetables I would grow.

To make the garden, I hoed the hard dirt. Next, I spread a layer of rich topsoil that smelled like mushrooms in a damp woods. Finally, I formed long rows with a shovel and scooped out quarter-sized holes with a spade. After placing a few seeds in each hole, I covered the seeds with black dirt. When a seed packet was empty, I put it on a stick and left it as a label at the end of the row.

For weeks, I waited patiently. Spring rains fell. Warm sun heated the ground. Finally, early one morning, I spotted a few tiny green shoots.

Nearly every day, I weeded, watered, or fertilized my garden. I loved spending time in the rows, smelling the fresh earth, and looking for new growth. By the middle of the summer, most of my vegetables were ripe. I harvested cucumbers, green beans, zucchini, and peppers. At the end of the summer, I picked bright red tomatoes right from the vine.

In early fall, my pumpkins started to appear. They looked like green balloons on the sprawling vines. I asked Dad to help me pick one special pumpkin.

"Kyle, how much does this thing weigh?" Dad asked. He groaned as he helped me lift it.

My pumpkin was so large that Dad suggested I enter it in the local Harvest Fair. Judges weighed and measured my big orange pumpkin, and I won a prize. My pumpkin and my garden made me feel very proud!

USING GRAPHIC ORGANIZERS

Before you write, use graphic organizers to help yourself think about, gather, and arrange details for your personal narrative.

The writer of the personal narrative on page 86 might have used a 5 Ws Chart, such as the one below.

Who?	Kyle (me), my father
What?	plant a garden, harvest the vegetables, grow a prize-winning pumpkin
Where?	my backyard garden
When?	spring, summer, early fall
Why?	I did it myself, I enjoyed cultivating a garden, I won a prize for my efforts

A 5 Ws Chart helps writers gather details that answer these questions: Who besides me was involved? What happened? Where and when did events take place? Why is this experience meaningful?

The writer of the personal narrative on page 86 might also have used a Time Line such as the one below. If you had been the writer, what steps involved in planting a garden would you have listed? Fill in the time line, writing the steps in the appropriate order. Some steps may have more than one part.

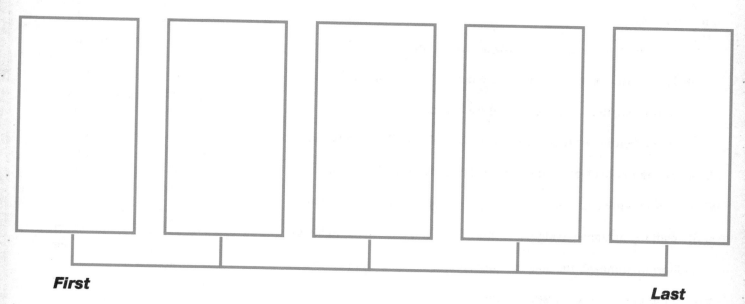

First

Last

A Time Line helps writers keep track of events or steps and the order in which they happen.

TAKING A LOOK AT PERSONAL NARRATIVES

Score:
4

Read the personal narrative below, which was written in response to the prompt on page 86. Read the comments and think about why this story scored a 4.

1

Stagestruck

Last summer I went to drama camp. We did voice exercises, acted in skits, wrote our own plays, and even designed and sewed simple costumes.

One day Jess my acting coach, announced, "We're going to perform a short play at the end of camp." She handed out copies of *Planet Alien*. Quickly, I looked at the cast of characters. Which role would I get? Would I be an alien child, the maid, the hero, the thief, or the sheriff? Then Jess assigned the roles. I would play the alien sheriff. I read the play carefully. To memorize my part, I wrote out my lines on index cards. I went over them again and again because I wanted to be perfect in my first play.

For the next few weeks, my fellow actors and me rehearsed. First, we rehearsed different scenes. Then we rehearsed the whole play from start to finish. Finally, we had several dress rehearsals.

The night before our first performance, I could hardly sleep because I kept hearing my lines echo in my head. Then it was the big night. When I got into my costume and makeup, I really looked like an alien sheriff with my antennae, badge, and laser-beam holster. As the lights in the auditorium dimmed, the audience turned silent. The curtain parted. "You're on! Go!" hissed the stage manager.

I strutted to the center of the stage. For a minute, I couldn't remember my first line. Then I said, "Now hold on there, you. I'm the law in this town." The audience laughed, I loved it, and I was stagestruck!

Your Turn

Now it's your turn to help the writer. Find and fix the errors in the writing. Go back to the pages in green if you need help.

1. Find and fix the **appositive** that is missing a **comma**. See pp. 38–39.

2. Find and fix the error in **subject pronoun** use. See pp. 10–11.

4

TEACHER COMMENTS

▲ Your title gives me a clue about what to expect. Thanks!

▲ You use a consistent point of view and effective transitional words to connect ideas.

▲ The realistic details and dialogue make the experience come to life.

▲ Your thoughts and feelings are expressed well. I sympathize with your first-night jitters!

▲ Your sentences are clear, complete, and varied.

▲ You've organized your narrative well. It has a clear beginning, middle, and ending. I like the way you linked the title to the ending.

3

PARTNER COMMENTS

2

Your story was fun to read. I even learned a little bit about acting.

Read the personal narrative and the comments that follow. Think about why this story scored a 3.

How I Got Over Stage Fright

I was in drama class at the rec center this summer. We had an acting coach. She taught us how to move on stage, how to "throw" our voices, and learning lines of dialogue. In the morning, we broke into groups. In order to write our own skits.

At the end of summer camp, our acting coach told us we were going to perform a whole play. The play was called *planet Alien*. It had weird characters like an alien maid. There was also an alien butler. I wanted to play the alien criminal.

I was assigned the part of the alien sheriff, the sheriff's costume consisted of a laser, a badge, a vest, and a large hat. I looked like a normal sheriff except for my large antennae and green makeup.

On opening night, I listened to the audience murmuring, the bernhardt auditorium was packed. When it was time for me to go on, I moved like a robot to the center of the stage. Then I completely went blank, but the stage manager whispered the lines.

"Hey pardner," I said to a human character named Moe, We don't want your kind around here."

The audience laughed, and my parents laughed the loudest. This is how I got over my stage fright and caught the acting bug.

Your Turn

Now it's your turn to help the writer. Find and fix the errors in the writing. Go back to the pages in green if you need help.

1. Find and fix the error in **parallel structure**. See pp. 42–43.
2. Find and fix the **sentence fragment**. See pp. 34–35.
3. Find and fix the three **capitalization errors**. See pp. 48–51.
4. Find and fix the two **run-on sentences**. See pp. 40–41.
5. Find and fix the missing **quotation marks**. See pp. 56–57.

TEACHER COMMENTS

▲ Your story has a title that captures readers' interest. Good.

▲ You tell the story consistently from your point of view. You could add more information about your thoughts and feelings to bring your point of view more sharply into focus, though.

▲ You include specific words like *throw, skits,* and *audience.* You could, however, replace more vague words with precise ones. For example, use *howled* instead of *laughed.*

▲ Although you use a few compound and complex sentences, most of your sentences are simple. Try varying your sentence **structure** by **combining** short, choppy **sentences**. See pp. 30–31, 34–39, and 44–45 for help.

▲ The beginning of your story is a bit weak, but I love the ending. Nice job!

PARTNER COMMENTS

You followed the prompt, but your story needed more details to really grab my interest. You could have used more dialogue too.

Score:
2

Read the personal narrative and the comments that follow. Think about why this story scored a 2.

1

I learned things in drama camp. Our acting coach taught us stuff. After a few weeks. We got parts in a play. We read lines. Then we had to practice. The night of the performance I felt scared. Their was a huge audience. All of my friends were there and so were my classmates and my family was in the front row.

Some of the characters in the play was aliens. One was a sheriff or some law person and his job was to catch humans and aliens who broke the law and he was the character I played in the play.

My knees was shaking when the curtain went up. I had to go to the center of the stage. I could almost not stand up. I was really scared. Then I spoked my lines. My coach smiled. My parents laughed. My friends laughs were even pretty loud. I felt proud and smiling. Because of my accomplishment.

2

PARTNER COMMENTS

Your story had a weak beginning and middle. The order of events was hard to follow. There weren't enough details to get me interested.

Your Turn

Now it's your turn to help the writer. Find and fix the errors in the writing. Go back to the pages in green if you need help.

1. Find and fix the two **sentence fragments**. See pp. 34–35.
2. Find and fix the one incorrect **homophone**. See pp. 28–29.
3. Find and fix the two **rambling sentences**. See pp. 40–41.
4. Find and fix the two errors in **subject-verb agreement**. See pp. 18–21.
5. Find and fix the incorrect **past-tense verb**. See pp. 16–17.
6. Find and fix the incorrect **possessive noun**. See pp. 8–9.
7. Find and fix the sentence that lacks **parallel structure**. See pp. 42–43.

4

TEACHER COMMENTS

▲ Please add a title to your story.
▲ You could add more details, and you could use some **dialogue**, too. See pp. 56–57 for help.
▲ Some parts of your story don't follow a logical order.
▲ Replace vague words like *stuff* and *got* with more **precise words**. See pp. 4–5 and 22–27.
▲ Avoid using **unnecessary words** or **phrases** such as *in the play*. See pp. 42–43.
▲ **Vary** the **structure** of your **sentences** for variety. See pp. 44–45.

3

Score: **1**

Read the personal narrative and the comments that follow. Think about why this story scored a 1.

1

Some actors are real talented. I want to be an actor someday one time I took acting classes I learned a lot. My class did a play. I was the sheriff. From another planet. Some of the kids in my class was already good actors. It was all new to me. Actors learn how to use they're voices. They learn how to make funny or sad faces. They learn how to move on a stage and using props. I felt week on the stage. What is the most important thing, that I learned? I found out that it is hard to learn lines. Maybe Ill be a famous actor. When I grow up.

PARTNER COMMENTS

2

Your story needs a title. I'm not exactly sure what accomplishment you're proud of. It was hard to follow your story because the events were mixed up.

TEACHER COMMENTS

3

▲ Your story should focus on a personal accomplishment. Please follow the prompt.

▲ To develop your story, add some characters and dialogue. Include a clear chain of events.

▲ Try using a logical pattern of organization, such as chronological order, to organize your narrative. It is hard to follow.

▲ Your **main ideas and details** should be more closely related. See pp. 58–59 for help.

▲ Use some **transitional words** or **phrases** to help readers follow the connections between ideas. See pp. 60–61.

▲ Try using some **vivid, colorful words** to create a stronger impression of the story events. See pp. 4–5 and 22–27.

Your Turn

Now it's your turn to help the writer. Find and fix the errors in the writing. Go back to the pages in green if you need help.

1. Indent the **paragraph**. See pp. 58–59.

2. Find and fix the **adjective** that should be an **adverb**. See pp. 26–27.

3. Find and fix the **run-on sentence**. See pp. 40–41.

4. Find and fix the two **sentence fragments**. See pp. 34–35.

5. Find and fix the error in **subject-verb agreement**. See pp. 18–21.

6. Find and fix the two incorrect **homophones**. See pp. 28–29.

7. Find and fix the error in **parallel structure**. See pp. 42–43.

8. Find and fix the **comma** that is used incorrectly with an **essential clause**. See pp. 52–53.

9. Find and fix the **contraction** error. See pp. 54–55.

4

USING A RUBRIC TO SCORE PERSONAL NARRATIVES

This rubric is based on a point scale of 1 to 4. It was used to score the personal narratives on pages 88–91. Use this rubric to remember what is important in personal narratives.

4

A score of 4 means that the writer

- ❑ connects the writing directly to the prompt.
- ❑ almost always uses the correct forms of words.
- ❑ almost always uses capitalization and punctuation correctly.
- ❑ almost always uses clear and complete sentences and includes sentence variety.
- ❑ uses precise words and effective transitional words to connect ideas.
- ❑ creates an engaging title that relates to the story.
- ❑ creates a clear beginning, middle, and ending.
- ❑ tells the story from his or her point of view and is clearly part of the story.
- ❑ provides many interesting story details, including thoughts and feelings.
- ❑ includes dialogue.
- ❑ begins a new paragraph for each change of idea or speaker.

2

A score of 2 means that the writer

- ❑ connects the writing to the prompt in a general way.
- ❑ uses some incorrect forms of words.
- ❑ makes some errors in capitalization or punctuation.
- ❑ uses little sentence variety.
- ❑ uses some run-on or rambling sentences or sentence fragments.
- ❑ uses mostly simple words and few transitional words.
- ❑ creates a title.
- ❑ creates a weak beginning, middle, or ending.
- ❑ usually tells the story from his or her point of view.
- ❑ provides few effective story details.
- ❑ includes little or no dialogue.
- ❑ may make some paragraphing errors.

3

A score of 3 means that the writer

- ❑ connects the writing to the prompt.
- ❑ usually uses the correct forms of words.
- ❑ usually uses capitalization and punctuation correctly.
- ❑ usually uses clear and complete sentences and includes some sentence variety.
- ❑ uses some precise words and some transitional words.
- ❑ creates a title that relates generally to the story.
- ❑ creates a beginning, middle, and ending.
- ❑ tells the story from his or her point of view.
- ❑ provides some interesting story details, including some thoughts and feelings.
- ❑ includes some dialogue.
- ❑ usually begins a new paragraph for each change of idea or speaker.

1

A score of 1 means that the writer

- ❑ does not successfully connect the writing to the prompt.
- ❑ uses many incorrect forms of words.
- ❑ makes many errors in capitalization or punctuation.
- ❑ uses almost no sentence variety.
- ❑ uses many run-on or rambling sentences or sentence fragments.
- ❑ uses simple or inappropriate words and very few transitional words.
- ❑ creates a weak title or has no title at all.
- ❑ creates an unclear beginning, middle, or ending.
- ❑ does not tell the story from his or her point of view or switches the point of view.
- ❑ provides weak or confusing story details.
- ❑ does not include dialogue or uses it incorrectly.
- ❑ may make many paragraphing errors.

SCORING PERSONAL NARRATIVES

Now it's your turn to score some personal narratives. The four personal narratives on pages 93 and 94 were written in response to this prompt.

> *Write about something that surprised you.*

Read each personal narrative. Write a few comments about it and then give it a score from 1 to 4. Think about what you've learned in this lesson as you match each story with its correct score.

Model A

Score: ▽

A Squeaky Present

Just before my birthday, my family spent a day at a farm. Poppy stopped on the way home at a store and bought some chicken wire. The rest of us waited in the car. Suddenly, I heard a soft squeaking sound.

"Mom, what's that noise?" I asked.

"Oh, its nothing," she said, chuckling. "Better check the springs when we get home, Jack," she said to my father.

I forgot about the noise. Squeaking away in the trunk. A few days later, I raced downstairs in view of the fact that it was my birthday. I couldnt wait to open my birthday presents. I saw a cardboard box that wasn't wrapped. I peeked inside and saw three yellow ducklings. "So that was the squeaking!" I exclaimed.

Comments:_____
_____
_____
_____
_____
_____
_____
_____

Model B

Score: ▽

One time my family went to a farm. Me and my brother went on a hayride and milked cows. When we drove home, dad maked a stop along the way. Dusty and me heard a noise in the trunk, it sounded like rusted springs. I asked my father what we should due. Mom laughed Dad told us not to worry. A few days after that, I ran downstairs on account of the fact that it was my birthday. I seen my presents. Right there on top of the big table. I opened one big cardboard box. Three ducks were inside. They were quacking up a storm. Ill never forget that birthday gift.

Comments:_____
_____
_____
_____
_____
_____
_____
_____

Model C

Score:

One day my family went to a farm in the country. We seen cows and chickens. There was also some horses and sheep. The tractor ride through the fields were the most funnest. After our day at the farm Dad drove home on a winding rode. My Brother and me heard a noise. From the trunk. We asked what it was. Dad said dont worry about it. A few days later I got a birthday present my parents gave me a box of ducks they quacked and quacked.

*Comments:*_____
_____
_____
_____
_____
_____
_____
_____

Model D

Score:

The Surprise in the Trunk

When I was a child, my parents took my brother and I to a farm. At the end of the day, Pop stopped at a hardware store near our home. Suddenly, I heard a weird noise from the back of the car. It was a squeaking noise.

"Did you hear that?" I asked my little brother.

"Hear what?" Dusty answered.

"That!" I shouted, hearing the squeaking again.

My mother chuckled. I asked her if something was wrong with the car, but she just shook her head.

After Pop returned, I told him about the noise in the trunk. To me, it sounded like rusty springs on an old toy. "Don't worry. I'll take care of it on your birthday," he said.

A few days later, I heard the squeaking noise again. I raced downstairs and saw a cardboard box. Inside, I found three fuzzy yellow ducklings quacking in a chorus. Somehow, my parents had managed to keep my squeaky birthday present a secret.

*Comments:*_____
_____
_____
_____
_____
_____
_____

WRITING A PERSONAL NARRATIVE

Now you get to write your own personal narrative. Use the prompt below.

> *Write about a time in your life when you learned an important lesson.*

Making Connections

- A personal narrative is a form of autobiography, or writing about your own life. Look at some autobiographies by well-known people such as Maya Angelou and Anne Frank to see what kinds of experiences they wrote about and how they wrote about them.

- Make a scrapbook of important events in your life. Include photographs, ticket stubs, pictures from magazines, newspaper articles, and so on. Write captions to explain each item. You can use the events included in your scrapbook to spark ideas for personal narratives.

- Keep a journal. Write notes about interesting things that happen to you during the course of a day, a week, or a month. Did you learn something new? Did you help someone you know? Your journal may be a source of ideas for future stories.

When You Write Your Personal Narrative

1. **Think about** what you want to write. Ask yourself some questions.
   - Who else besides me is involved?
   - Where and when does the story take place?
   - What are the most important events in the story?
   - Why was this experience meaningful to me?
   - How does the story end?

   Use graphic organizers to gather and sort the information.

2. **Write** your first draft. Be sure your story has a clear beginning, middle, and ending.

3. **Read** your draft. Use the checklist that your teacher will give you to review your writing.

4. **Edit** your story. Make changes until the setting and characters are clear and strong and the plot makes sense and is easy to follow.

5. **Proofread** your story one last time.

6. **Write** a neat copy of your story and give it to your partner.

Work with a Partner

7. **Read** your partner's personal narrative.

8. **Score** your partner's story from 1 to 4, using the rubric on page 92. Then complete the Partner Comments sheet that your teacher will give you. Tell what you like about the story and what you think would make it better.

9. **Switch** papers.

10. **Think about** your partner's comments. Read your story again. Make changes that you think will improve your personal narrative.

11. **Write** a neat final copy of your personal narrative.

FICTIONAL NARRATIVES

A fictional narrative is a story that is not true. It comes from your imagination. It is usually about characters that you invent. A fictional narrative may be set in any time or place.

Here is a sample writing prompt for a fictional narrative.

> *Write a story about a character who lives in the past or in the future.*

Read this fictional narrative, which was written in response to the prompt. Then read the Writing Tips to learn more about fictional narratives.

Writing Tips

Fictional Narratives have these important features.

Story Structure

The title should get readers interested in the story.

Beginning
* Setting: the time and place of the story
* Characters: the people or animals in the story, usually one main character along with other characters who work with or against the main character
* Problem or Conflict: a problem or situation that the characters must deal with or solve

Middle
* Plot Events: the events that make up the action of the story, showing how the characters deal with the problem. The plot events are presented in a logical order and include a climax or turning point, the high point of interest where the plot events begin to turn toward the resolution.

Ending
* Resolution: how the characters resolve the conflict; ties up loose ends of story

Dialogue: words the characters say

Narrator: the "voice" telling the story

Imagery: descriptive details, sensory words, and comparisons that make the story come alive for readers

Westward Ho!

The wagon bumped along the dusty trail. Suddenly, Mr. Sampson pulled the reins to stop the horses.

"Why did we stop, Pa?" Aaron asked.

"I don't know, Son. Maybe there's a broken wagon wheel up ahead," Pa said.

Then Ben, a boy from another wagon, came running.

"Hello, Aaron! Did you hear? Greeley Holmes has cholera," Ben said.

Aaron knew that cholera was serious. Many settlers traveling along the Oregon Trail died from cholera. Aaron went to tell his mother the bad news.

"Aaron, please get me some water. The baby is burning up," Ma said.

Aaron's mother pressed a cold cloth on Matilda's forehead. Aaron didn't say a word. Did Matilda have cholera, too?

The entire wagon train stopped for the night. The covered wagons were placed in a circle, with the animals in the middle. Aaron helped his father make a campfire. Soon the women were boiling tea and cooking supper. After trying to eat, Aaron pushed away his plate of rice with dried beef.

"Don't you want to sing tonight, Aaron?" Pa asked.

"No, Pa," Aaron replied.

Aaron paced. Ma approached, looking worried.

"Aaron, go fetch Doc Wrigley," Ma said quietly.

Aaron found Doc Wrigley. The doc examined the baby and then disappeared into the night. Aaron's heart pounded.

"Ma, how's Matilda?" Aaron asked. He was afraid to hear the news.

"She's just fine, Aaron. She has a slight case of sunburn," Ma said.

With a sigh of relief, Aaron joined the others at the campfire and began to sing at the top of his lungs.

USING GRAPHIC ORGANIZERS

Before you begin to write, use graphic organizers to plan and arrange details for your story.

The writer of the fictional narrative on page 96 might have used a Setting Chart such as the one below.

A Setting Chart helps writers gather and organize specific details about where and when a story takes place.

The writer of the story on page 96 also might have used a Story Map to plot the elements of the story. If you had been the writer, how would you have used the map? Complete the Story Map with details about the story.

A Story Map helps writers organize details for a story.

"Westward Ho!"
SETTING
Time: Place:
CHARACTERS
Main Character:
Other Characters:
PROBLEM:
PLOT EVENTS
Event 1:
Event 2:
Event 3:
Event 4:
Climax:
RESOLUTION:

Score:

4

Read the fictional narrative below, which was written in response to the prompt on page 96. Read the comments and think about why this story scored a 4.

1

How Not to Use Your Robot

Selena Delray hated housework. She didn't want to dust the family rocket ship, vacuum the time capsule, or scrubbing the sleeping chamber. As her pet robot wandered past, Selena had a great idea.

"I'll hook up Howie to my cleaning program," she murmured.

Selena fitted Howie with cleaning tools. She adjusted his computer chip and downloaded some cleaning software. Immediately, Howie kicked up a cloud of dirt and dust.

"Hey, Howie, slow down"! said Selena.

Before long, Howie had knocked over stainless steel flowers, had broken antique compact disks, and had shredded some expensive climate-controlled outfits in the closet.

"Selena, what happened?" gasped her mom. "The nutrition unit is a mess, and my valuable music recordings from the 21st century are ruined," she cried.

"Oh, Mum, I'm so sorry. Howie did it!" Selena exclaimed.

"Howie? He's only programmed to stand at the door, bark, and roll over," responded Mrs. Delray.

Howie whirled past, humming and hissing.

"Selena, stop him!" her mother shouted.

Selena said sternly, "Howie, sit! Stay!"

Howie sat and didn't move. Selena reversed everything she had done, hoping that Howie would be back to his old self. Sure enough, he was.

"I'll never do that again!" vowed Selena.

Your Turn

Now it's your turn to help the writer. Find and fix the errors in the writing. Go back to the pages in green if you need help.

1. Find and fix the error in **parallel structure**. See pp. 42–43.

2. Find and fix the mistake in the use of **end punctuation** with **quotation marks**. See pp. 56–57.

TEACHER COMMENTS

4

▲ Your title gives me a clue about what to expect. Good.

▲ The plot events unfold in a logical way. You use descriptive details and dialogue to create believable characters in a futuristic setting.

▲ You keep a consistent narrative voice throughout. Good!.

▲ Your story has a clear beginning, middle, and ending. You include a strong turning point, with Mrs. Delray saying, "Selena, stop him!"

PARTNER COMMENTS

3

2

I liked the funny characters and the unusual setting in your story. It made me laugh.

Read this fictional narrative and the comments that follow. Think about why this story scored a 3.

1

Robot Blues

Selena Delray had a pet robot named Howie. One day Selena decided she didn't want to do the housework. She made some adjustments to the robot. Howie became a sort of maid robot, he was programmed to clean, dust, and vacuum. The only problem was that Howie started breaking things and making a mess. Howie pulled things off shelves, knocked over valuable antiques, and whirling around in circles. Howie sent up clouds of dust wherever he went.

When she came in the door. Mrs. Delray asked Selena what was going on. Selena told her that she had done her chores with Howies help. Selena admitted that this had been a bad idea.

"You're right!" exclaimed Mrs. Delray. "Just look at this place!"

Selena couldn't get Howie to stop. Until she offered him a computer floppy disk as a treat. Howie paused long enough for Selena to reprogram him. Howie barked and ran around. He acted like an ordinary pet robot again.

Selena started cleaning up the mess, it would take a long time. She swept up the pieces of a frame that held an old photograph with a frown. She dusted the dirty metal furniture.

"I'll do my own chores from now on!" Selena declared.

Your Turn

Now it's your turn to help the writer. Find and fix the errors in the writing. Go back to the pages in green if you need help.

1. Find and fix the two **run-on sentences**. See pp. 40–41.
2. Find and fix the error in **parallel structure**. See pp. 42–43.
3. Find and fix the two **sentence fragments**. See pp. 34–35.
4. Find and fix the incorrect **possessive noun**. See pp. 8–9.
5. Find and fix the **misplaced modifier**. See pp. 32–33.

TEACHER COMMENTS

4

▲ Your story has an interesting title.

▲ Your story does include characters and a setting, but you could add more **dialogue** for interest. See pp. 56–57 for help.

▲ Try **combining** some short, related **sentences**. See pp. 30–31, 34–39, and 44–45.

▲ Add some **transitional words** and **phrases** to more clearly connect the sequence of events in the plot. See pp. 60–61.

▲ The ending of your story is very effective. Good work!

2

PARTNER COMMENTS

3

I could tell that your story was about the future, and I liked the robot Howie. It was a good story.

Score:
2

Read this fictional narrative and the comments that follow.
Think about why this story scored a 2.

Your Turn

1

About a Robot

A girl named Selena didn't like to clean, she wanted her pet robot to clean instead. She figured out a way for the robot to help her. Selena let the robot due all of her chores.

When Selena's mother came home, she was angry. She seen dirt and dust everywhere. The house was a mess on account of the fact because the robot was out of control. It broke things but Selena couldn't make it stop and so she tried to pull its wires.

Selena guest she had to clean up all by herself. The robot had leaved a big mess. Selena had to put everything back. Because of that robot! Selena was mad! She thought the pet robot would help her instead she worked more harder than ever before. Not what she had planned!

Now it's your turn to help the writer. Find and fix the errors in the writing. Go back to the pages in green if you need help.

1. Find and fix the two **run-on sentences**.
   See pp. 40–41.
2. Find and fix the two incorrect **homophones**.
   See pp. 28–29.
3. Find and fix the two incorrect **past-tense verbs**.
   See pp. 16–17.
4. Find and fix the **unnecessary phrase**.
   See pp. 42–43.
5. Find and fix the **rambling sentence**.
   See pp. 40–41.
6. Find and fix the two **sentence fragments**.
   See pp. 34–35.
7. Find and fix the **double comparison**.
   See pp. 24–25.

TEACHER COMMENTS

4

▲ Please add a title that gives a little more information about your story.

▲ Your story does have a beginning, middle, and ending, but I think you should flesh out your story by providing more information about the main character, setting, and plot. For example, you might create another character for Selena to work with or against. Also, how did Selena resolve the problem with the robot?

▲ Add some **dialogue** to make Selena come to life. Punctuate the dialogue correctly. See pp. 56–57 for help.

▲ Use some **sensory words** to create imagery that will help readers visualize your story. See pp. 58–59.

▲ Use more **variety** in the **structure** of your **sentences** to add more depth to your story. See pp. 44–45.

2

PARTNER COMMENTS

If your story had more details, I could picture the characters and the setting better. Some of the events were a little confusing too.

3

Read this fictional narrative and the comments that follow. Think about why this story scored a 1.

Although she did laundry this girl didn't like to clean or dusting. She had a robot. She wanted her robot to help her clean the house and she tried to make the robot help her and the girls mother got mad at her. She could not bare it. Because it was the robot who had messed the house. The robot starts acting weird, and smoke came out of the head and eyes. The wires in the robot was on fire. Suddenly the robot was totally out of control and the girl couldn't figure out what to do, and she got mad. Vases and pictures are falling down, and the girl yelled. The girl got the Robot to stop. After it had made a big mess.

2

PARTNER COMMENTS

Your story needs a title, a better main character, and more description. What is the girl's name? Your story didn't have enough details, so I couldn't follow the plot very well.

3

TEACHER COMMENTS

▲ Please add a title that tells something about your story.

▲ A fictional narrative should include well developed characters, a setting that readers can picture in their minds, and a series of events that involve a problem and its resolution. Please follow the prompt.

▲ Your story needs a stronger beginning, middle, and ending. Work on arranging a series of related plot events in chronological order. Also, watch out for unrelated **details**. See pp. 58–59 for help.

▲ Use some vivid **sensory words** and descriptive language to create a stronger impression of the events. See pp. 58–59.

▲ A fictional narrative should include **dialogue**. Add some conversation between characters, and make sure you punctuate the dialogue correctly. See pp. 56–57.

4

Your Turn

Now it's your turn to help the writer. Find and fix the errors in the writing. Go back to the pages in green if you need help.

1. Find and fix the **introductory independent clause** that is missing a **comma**. See pp. 52–53.

2. Find and fix the error in **parallel structure**. See pp. 42–43.

3. Find and fix the two **rambling sentences**. See pp. 40–41.

4. Find and fix the incorrect **possessive noun**. See pp. 8–9.

5. Find and fix the incorrect **homophone**. See pp. 28–29.

6. Find and fix the two **sentence fragments**. See pp. 34–35.

7. Find and fix the two **inconsistent verb tenses**. See pp. 42–43.

8. Find and fix the error in **subject-verb agreement**. See pp. 18–21.

9. Find and fix the **capitalization** error. See pp. 50–51.

USING A RUBRIC TO SCORE FICTIONAL NARRATIVES

This rubric is based on a point scale of 1 to 4. It was used to score the fictional narratives on pages 98–101. Use this rubric to remember what is important in fictional narratives.

4 A score of 4 means that the writer

- ❏ connects the writing directly to the prompt.
- ❏ almost always uses the correct forms of words.
- ❏ almost always uses capitalization and punctuation correctly.
- ❏ almost always uses clear and complete sentences and includes sentence variety.
- ❏ creates a catchy title that relates to the story.
- ❏ uses many interesting words and details.
- ❏ creates a clear beginning, middle, and ending.
- ❏ develops a clear setting, one or more believable characters, and an active plot that includes a problem and a resolution.
- ❏ uses dialogue to make the characters come alive.
- ❏ keeps the narrative voice consistent.
- ❏ begins a new paragraph for each change of idea or speaker.

2 A score of 2 means that the writer

- ❏ connects the writing to the prompt in a general way.
- ❏ uses some incorrect forms of words.
- ❏ uses some incorrect capitalization or punctuation.
- ❏ uses little sentence variety.
- ❏ uses some run-on or rambling sentences or sentence fragments.
- ❏ creates a title that relates somewhat to the story.
- ❏ uses mostly simple words and details.
- ❏ creates a weak beginning, middle, or ending.
- ❏ fails to clearly develop setting, characters, or plot.
- ❏ uses little or no dialogue.
- ❏ may sometimes switch the narrative voice.
- ❏ may make some paragraphing errors.

3 A score of 3 means that the writer

- ❏ connects the writing to the prompt.
- ❏ usually uses the correct forms of words.
- ❏ usually uses capitalization and punctuation correctly.
- ❏ usually uses clear and complete sentences and includes some sentence variety.
- ❏ creates a title that relates generally to the story.
- ❏ uses some interesting words and details.
- ❏ creates a beginning, middle, and ending.
- ❏ develops a setting, one or more characters, and a plot.
- ❏ uses some dialogue between characters.
- ❏ usually keeps the narrative voice consistent.
- ❏ usually begins a new paragraph for each change of idea or speaker.

1 A score of 1 means that the writer

- ❏ does not successfully connect the writing to the prompt.
- ❏ uses many incorrect forms of words.
- ❏ often uses incorrect capitalization or punctuation.
- ❏ uses almost no sentence variety.
- ❏ uses several run-on or rambling sentences or sentence fragments.
- ❏ creates a poor title or has no title at all.
- ❏ uses very simple words and details.
- ❏ creates an unclear beginning, middle, or ending.
- ❏ fails to present or develop setting, characters, or plot.
- ❏ does not include any dialogue or uses it incorrectly.
- ❏ may often switch the narrative voice.
- ❏ may make many paragraphing errors.

SCORING FICTIONAL NARRATIVES

Now it's your turn to score some fictional narratives. The four fictional narratives on pages 103 and 104 were written in response to this prompt.

> *Write a story about characters who face a crisis.*

Read each fictional narrative. Write a few comments about it. Then give it a score from 1 to 4. Think about what you've learned in this lesson as you match each story with its correct score.

Model A

Score: ▽

A Scary Day at School
Jamal Williams was doing math when it went dark.
"Keep going, class," said Mrs. Labar, Jamals teacher.
Everyone kept working. Although it was getting darker. Another teacher spoke to Mrs. Labar.
"Class, I've just found out that there is a huge blackout, the entire city is without power. We'll stay here until it is safe for school to be dismissed," Mrs. Labar said.
One kid started to cry. Another brought the class from the cafeteria some food. Jamal didn't feel hungry. He just wanted to go home. He wondered if his brother was scared.
Kids played games, did homework, and ate snacks. Finally, the lights came on. Everyone cheered.
When Jamal got home, he was very happy as he turned on the hall light.

Comments:_____
_____
_____
_____
_____
_____
_____

Model B

Score: ▽

One day the schools lights went out. The city was dark and there was no electricity so subways and buses couldn't run. It was spooky. When you walked outside. no one could see there books. A boy was taking a math test. He couldn't see good, and he felt real nervous. The teacher told everyone to stay calm. They would have to wait at school. Until crews maked the electricity work again. Some students in the class was hungry and they wanted snacks. Then everyone could go home. Lights in the city was on again.

Comments:_____
_____
_____
_____
_____
_____
_____

Model C

Score: ▽

Jamal was doing math. When the lights went out. It was real hard to see.

Another teacher knocked on the door. She speaked to Jamals teacher. The teacher looked upset.

The city has no electricity, the teacher said.

All of the students in the class was scared. They couldn't finish there tests. They had snacks and looked out the windows. At the quiet city below. Some kids played games. Others talked quietly. Pretty soon the lights went on. In the school and in the city. Everyone was allowed to go home finally. It was over.

*Comments:*_____
_____
_____
_____
_____
_____
_____
_____

Model D

Score: ▽

Blackout

Jamal was doing math when the room went black.

"Hey, what's going on?" one student said.

Mrs. Labar said, "Now don't panic. Stay in your seats. We must have had a power outage."

Everyone sat silently. Soon, another teacher came in and whispered to Mrs. Labar.

"Class, the entire city is without electricity," said Mrs. Labar. "We will have to stay here until the power is restored and it's safe for you to leave school."

Jamal thought about baseball practice that afternoon. It would probably be cancelled.

"When do you think we can go home?" Jackie, a new student, asked worriedly.

"I honestly don't know, Jackie. The city is in a state of emergency," said Mrs. Labar.

The class past the time by singing songs, playing games, and doing some homework. Then, all of a sudden, the lights hummed on.

"Yeah!" cheered the entire class.

After dismissal, Jamal and some friends walked home safely together.

*Comments:*_____
_____
_____
_____
_____
_____
_____

WRITING A FICTIONAL NARRATIVE

Now you get to write your own fictional narrative. Use the prompt below.

> *Write a story about a character who did something brave.*

When You Write Your Fictional Narrative

1. **Think about** what you want to write. Ask yourself some questions.
   - Where and when will the story take place?
   - Who will be in the story?
   - What problem will the characters have to face?
   - How will the characters try to solve the problem?
   - How will the story end?

   Use graphic organizers to gather and sort the information.

2. **Write** your first draft. Make sure your fictional narrative has a clear beginning, middle, and ending.

3. **Read** your draft. Use the checklist that your teacher will give you to review your writing.

4. **Edit** your story. Make changes until the setting and characters are clear and the plot makes sense and is easy to follow.

5. **Proofread** your story one last time.

6. **Write** a neat copy of your story and give it to your partner.

Work with a Partner

7. **Read** your partner's story.

8. **Score** your partner's story from 1 to 4, using the rubric on page 102. Then complete the Partner Comments sheet that your teacher will give you. Tell what you like about the story and what you think would make it better.

9. **Switch** papers.

10. **Think about** your partner's comments. Read your story again. Make changes that you think will improve your fictional narrative.

11. **Write** a neat final copy of your fictional narrative.

Making Connections

- A fictional narrative can be a story about an imaginary character, or it can be an imaginary story about a real-life person. When you read about a past event in science or social studies, think about how to turn the event into a realistic fiction story. What would the setting be? Who would the characters be? What would the problem be? How would it be resolved?

- In your journal, write about interesting people you meet, conversations you overhear, places you visit, and different kinds of conflicts you encounter. Later you can use these notes to develop realistic characters, settings, dialogue, and plot events in stories you write.

- Who is your favorite author? Why do you like his or her stories? What kinds of characters, settings, and events does this author write about? When you read, think about what makes a good story.

An **expository essay** is a short paper that explains something. The main ideas and details may come from what you already know about the topic. Here is a sample writing prompt for an expository essay.

> *Write an essay explaining why you like your best friend.*

Read this expository essay, which was written in response to the prompt. Then read the Writing Tips to learn more about expository essays.

Writing Tips

* Think of an interesting title that tells about the topic of the essay and makes readers want to learn more.

* In your introductory paragraph, tell what the essay is about by providing a clear topic sentence that relates to the whole essay, not just the first paragraph. Also, catch readers' interest with a strong lead, such as a dramatic statement, a thought-provoking question, or an interesting quote.

* Use the middle, or body, of your essay to explain the topic. Include at least three main ideas about the topic and support each main idea with facts, examples, or reasons. These details may come from your own experiences or from outside sources.

* Although an expository essay is typically filled with facts, you can include a few supporting opinions.

* Present your ideas in a logical order, using appropriate transitions to make the ideas move smoothly from one to the next.

* Draw your essay to a conclusion by summing up the main ideas, restating the topic sentence in a different way, or giving an overview or a final thought. Don't introduce any new information in the conclusion, however.

Ashley, Superstar and Best Friend Ever

I love sports! To be my best friend, a person has to share this love totally. That's why Ashley is the perfect best friend for me. Not only does she love sports, but she's also a superstar and a nice one too.

In every sport, Ashley stands out above everyone else. It's been like that since we were four years old. Even then she could run faster than kids two and three years older than she was. Now she can plunk a softball into the outfield with ease and hit free-throw shots one right after another.

As we began to play organized sports, Ashley's natural talent really came out. Coaches singled her out for special instruction. She drew me into these extra sessions because we always did everything together. Whatever I've learned about sports, I've learned it with or from Ashley.

I've also learned how to be a better person because of Ashley. Last year after a car accident, I had to spend a month in bed. So that I wouldn't miss a minute of our softball season, Ashley had her dad videotape each game and practice. Every day after school, she came over so we could watch and analyze every game together.

I'll never be as good as Ashley at any sport, but I really don't mind. Ashley has always been a model for me. In sports, she is always trying. As a friend, she is always thoughtful and always there for me!

The main reason that I like my best friend Ashley is that she is a model athlete and a model friend.

USING GRAPHIC ORGANIZERS

You can use graphic organizers to gather, sort, and organize your ideas before writing your essay.

The writer of the expository essay on page 106 might have used a Character Trait Chart, such as the one below.

ASHLEY

Athlete
- superstar
- natural talent
- special instruction
- always trying
- a model

Friend
- nice
- sharing
- thoughtful
- always there
- a model

A Character Trait Chart helps writers identify and sort out important traits about a person who is the focus of an essay.

A Sequence Chart is another useful graphic organizer. How might the writer of the essay on page 106 have used this chart? Jot down a few words to fill in each box.

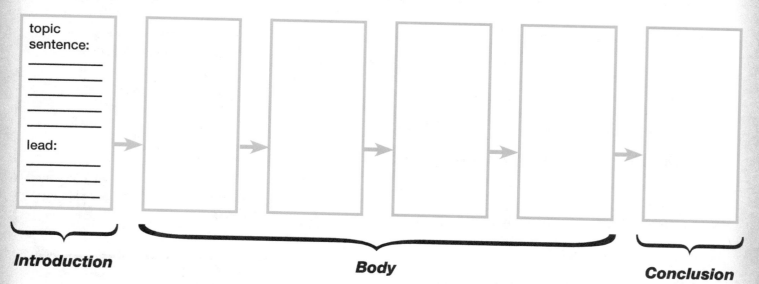

topic sentence:
_____
_____
_____
_____

lead:
_____
_____
_____

Introduction

Body

Conclusion

A Sequence Chart helps essay writers put ideas in a logical order.

Score: 4

Read the expository essay below, which was written in response to the prompt on page 106. Read the comments and think about why this essay scored a 4.

1

The Best Possible Friend for Me

Todd my best friend, is not a sports hero, a genius, or the funniest kid I know. My mom says Todd has a sunny disposition. Maybe that's what I like about him. Todd makes me feel happy because he's almost always happy.

You've probably seen that look on people's faces that says, "Watch out! I'm in an ugly mood!" I don't think I've ever seen that look on Todd's face. I've seen him angry, but his anger lasts only briefly. It is sort of like a summer thunderstorm.

In fact, the corners of Todd's mouth are usually turned slightly up as though whatever is happening is precisely right. He looks like he's enjoying himself all the time.

It's not that Todd is perfect. He's not. Like me, he's average in school. In sports, we're never picked first.

If a referee makes an unfair call or if a coach benches me, I'll complain loudly. Todd, on the other hand, will take his penalty with a shrug and move on. When I ask him how he can be so relaxed when something totally unfair happens to him, he says, "It's only a game.

I think that if you look up *happy* in a dictionary, you'll find Todd's picture. I like that about him, and we'll probably be best friends forever.

Your Turn

Now it's your turn to help the writer. Find and fix the errors in the writing. Go back to the pages in green if you need help.

1. Find and fix the **appositive** that is missing a **comma**. See pp. 38–39.

2. Find and fix missing **quotation marks**. See pp. 56–57.

TEACHER COMMENTS

4

▲ Your title and your opening paragraph, with the clear topic sentence, introduce me to the topic right away. You catch my interest by telling me up front what Todd is *not* like. Nice lead!

▲ I like the way you use the simile of the thunderstorm to describe Todd's anger.

▲ You do a nice job organizing your ideas into a clear beginning, middle, and ending. Your final observation is an effective conclusion.

▲ Thank you for adding variety to your sentences. Your writing is a pleasure to read.

PARTNER COMMENTS

3

2

Your essay made me realize how much a happy person can affect a friendship.

Read the expository essay and the comments that follow. Think about why this essay scored a 3.

Why Todd Is My Best Friend

Todd is my best friend. He's not a Sports hero, a genius, or the funniest kid I know. My mom thinks Todd has a sunny disposition. I like that about him. When him and I are together, I feel happy. I like that feeling.

Some peoples faces say "Don't get in my way." Todd doesn't ever look that way. He does get angry once in a while. Even then, it's over in a flash. Then he's happy again.

Look at the corners of Todd's mouth. You'll probably notice that they are curved in a smile. Todd always looks like he's enjoying himself. In addition, Todd has a real happy laugh. It makes everyone who hears it feel great.

Todd is not perfect. He and I are average in school. We're picked neither first nor last for teams. One day there was a real unfair call by the referee. I complained a lot. Another time the coach benched me. I complained then, too. Todd doesn't let things like that bother him. I asked Todd why he doesn't get upset. He doesn't really understand my problem. To him it's just a game. There's no reason to be upset.

Look up the word *happy* in a dictionary. I think you'll find Todd's picture there. I like that about him. Him and I will be best friends forever.

Your Turn

Now it's your turn to help the writer. Find and fix the errors in the writing. Go back to the pages in green if you need help.

1. Find and fix the **capitalization** error. See pp. 46–47.
2. Find and fix two incorrect **pronouns**. See pp. 10–11.
3. Find and fix the incorrect **possessive noun**. See pp. 8–9.
4. Find and fix the incorrect **punctuation** of a **direct quotation**. See pp. 56–57.
5. Find and fix two **adjectives** that should be **adverbs**. See pp. 26–27.

TEACHER COMMENTS — 4

▲ Your title and introductory paragraph connect to the prompt, introduce the topic, and get my interest.

▲ You use paragraphing well to organize your ideas into a logical order.

▲ Thank you for creating a clear conclusion that sums up your explanation of why Todd is your best friend.

▲ Your essay would be stronger if you **joined** some short, related **sentences** for variety. See pp. 30–31, 34–39, and 44–45 for help.

PARTNER COMMENTS — 3

2

I could tell why you like Todd from your details and words. More dialogue would have helped, though.

Score: **2**

Read the expository essay and the comments that follow. Think about why this essay scored a 2.

1

Best Friends

Todd is my best friend. I met him in second grade when we both have mrs. Reilly for a teacher. We went on the bus together. Todd was happy then, and he is still real happy.

Todds face is never mean. Like some kids faces are. Todd gets angry. Then he gets happy. That's just his way.

Look at Todd sometime. He smiles a lot. He laughs. Everyone who hears that laugh feel great. I get upset a lot. Not Todd. He doesn't get upset at unfair calls in Games. He thinks it is just a game. No reason to get upset. Todd is happy a lot. I like that about him. He is my best friend.

Your Turn

Now it's your turn to help the writer. Find and fix the errors in the writing. Go back to the pages in green if you need help.

1. Indent the **paragraph** that isn't indented. See pp. 58–59.
2. Find and fix the **inconsistent verb tense**. See pp. 42–43.
3. Find and fix the two **capitalization** errors. See pp. 46–47 and 50–51.
4. Find and fix the **adjective** that should be an **adverb**. See pp. 26–27.
5. Find and fix the two incorrect **possessive nouns**. See pp. 8–9.
6. Find and fix the three **sentence fragments**. See pp. 34–35.
7. Find and fix the error in **subject-verb agreement**. See pp. 20–21.

2

3

PARTNER COMMENTS

You used good details to explain why Todd is your best friend. You could have used better words and longer sentences, though.

TEACHER COMMENTS

4

▲ You should follow the prompt more closely and state your topic clearly at the beginning. You should focus on telling why you like Todd.

▲ You need to provide details that help your readers understand what you are explaining. Try to think of examples that would tell what Todd is like and how those aspects of Todd make you feel.

▲ Make sure your essay has a clear beginning, middle, and ending. You provide details, but you could develop them better.

▲ Read your essay aloud to see how it sounds. Use more **variety** in the **structure** and **type** of **sentences** you use. See pp. 30–31, 36–37, and 44–45 for help.

▲ More **precise words** would give your essay more impact. See pp. 4–5 and 22–27.

Score:
1

Read the expository essay and the comments that follow.
Think about why this essay scored a 1.

1

It is Todd. Todd and I was in second Grade together. We rode the School bus together. That there was when we met, Todd was happy even back then he made me happy and smiling too. Todd is happy, but he does get angry sometimes. The expressions on some kids faces is mean. Todds face never looks mean. We are OK at sports. We get OK grades at school. We are on teams together. Last year some coaches are unfair to us. I got upset about there calls. Todd was not upset. You guest it. Todd is the most happiest person I know. That makes me happy.

PARTNER COMMENTS

2

You made many errors, which made your essay hard to read. I had trouble understanding why Todd is your best friend because your ideas were so mixed up.

TEACHER COMMENTS

3

▲ The beginning of your essay should clearly indicate that Todd is your best friend. Reread the prompt and use that to help you write your introduction.

▲ You need to break more of your ideas into indented **paragraphs**. Make sure each paragraph has a different **main idea** with supporting **details**. See pp. 58–59 for help.

▲ Your ending is a little abrupt. You could give more information about why you like Todd.

▲ Your writing will be smoother and more enjoyable to read if you **join** some short **sentences** that have related ideas. See pp. 30–31 and 34–39.

4

Your Turn

Now it's your turn to help the writer. Find and fix the errors in the writing. Go back to the pages in green if you need help.

1. Find and fix the two errors in **subject-verb agreement**. See pp. 18–19.

2. Find and fix two **capitalization** errors See pp. 48–51.

3. Find and fix the **run-on sentence.** See pp. 40–41.

4. Find and fix the **unnecessary word**. See pp. 42–43.

5. Find and fix the error in **parallel construction**. See pp. 42–43.

6. Find and fix the two incorrect **possessive nouns**. See pp. 8–9.

7. Find and fix the **inconsistent verb tense**. See pp. 42–43.

8. Find and fix the two incorrect **homophones**. See pp. 28–29.

9. Find and fix the **double comparison**. See pp. 22–23.

USING A RUBRIC TO SCORE EXPOSITORY ESSAYS

This rubric is based on a point scale of 1 to 4. It was used to score the expository essays on pages 108–111. Use this rubric to remember what is important in expository essays.

4

A score of 4 means that the writer

- connects the writing directly to the prompt.
- almost always uses the correct forms of words.
- almost always uses capitalization and punctuation correctly.
- almost always uses clear and complete sentences and includes variety in sentences.
- uses effective words.
- creates a title that relates directly to the essay topic.
- clearly introduces the topic at the beginning.
- creates a strong beginning, middle, and ending.
- explains the topic with at least three main ideas along with relevant supporting details.
- presents the ideas in an order that creates an informative essay.
- begins a new paragraph for each change of idea.

2

A score of 2 means that the writer

- connects the writing to the prompt in a general way.
- uses some incorrect forms of words.
- uses some incorrect capitalization or punctuation.
- uses little variety in sentences.
- uses some run-on or rambling sentences or sentence fragments.
- uses mostly simple words.
- usually creates a title that relates in some way to the essay topic.
- presents the topic within the essay but uses too few main ideas or supporting details to fully explain the topic.
- creates a weak a beginning, middle, or ending.
- presents the ideas in a weak or choppy order.
- may make some paragraphing errors.

3

A score of 3 means that the writer

- connects the writing to the prompt.
- usually uses the correct forms of words.
- usually uses capitalization and punctuation correctly.
- usually uses clear and complete sentences and includes some variety in sentences.
- uses some effective words.
- creates a title that relates to the essay topic in a general way.
- introduces the topic toward the beginning.
- creates a beginning, middle, and ending.
- explains the topic with some main ideas along with some supporting details.
- presents the ideas in an order that makes sense.
- usually begins a paragraph for each change of idea.

1

A score of 1 means that the writer

- does not successfully connect the writing to the prompt.
- uses many incorrect forms of words.
- often uses incorrect capitalization or punctuation.
- uses almost no variety in sentences.
- uses several run-on or rambling sentences or sentence fragments.
- uses simple words.
- creates a poor title or has no title at all.
- includes a topic in the essay but uses too few main ideas or relevant supporting details to adequately explain the topic.
- creates an unclear beginning, middle, or ending.
- presents the ideas in an unclear manner.
- may make many paragraphing errors.

SCORING EXPOSITORY ESSAYS

Now it's your turn to score some expository essays. The four essays on pages 113 and 114 were written in response to this prompt.

> *Write an essay about three things you would want to have with you if you were stranded alone on a deserted island.*

Read each expository essay. Write a few comments about it. Then give it a score from 1 to 4. Think about what you've learned in this lesson as you match each essay with its correct score.

Model A

Score: ▽

Alone!

I am alone on a deserted island. I need to eat. I need to drink. I need to find a place to sleep. I need to stay safe. What do I need?

I need matches. I would chop wood and building a fire. Then I could make a smoke signal. I could cook my food.

A knife for cutting stuff. I might make a spear for fishing. Maybe one for hunting too. I would build a shelter.

I would collect water with them there bags. The bags could hold water too for drinking. I never sleeped on bags before but I think they would keep me warm.

Comments: _____

_____

_____

_____

_____

_____

_____

Model B

Score: ▽

It is hard to be on a Deserted Island all alone. First anyone there need to find a place to live. And things to eat and drink. Matches would help and a knife would help and some trash bags would help too. I would build a fire and cooking my food. Plants and fish is real good to eat except that you don't want to eat them raw which is why you need that fire. I would need a knifes sharp blades. I could cut stuff that I need. I would make a hut. I really wouldn't want to be alone on an island. That would be real scary.

Comments: _____

_____

_____

_____

_____

_____

_____

Model C

Score: ▽

Stranded on a Deserted Isle!

If I was alone on a deserted island, the three things I would want would be matches, a knife, and a box of plastic trash bags. I think these three items would assist my survival.

The matches would be used to obviously build a fire. With a fire I could warm myself, signal rescuers, and cook food. I could also scare away predators.

A knife would help me create tools with which I could hunt and prepare foods. I could also cut grasses and other vegetation for making mats and bowls.

With the plastic trash bags, I could build a shelter or a ground cover. The bags would provide warmth, and they are waterproof. I could also collect water in them.

With these three items, I could survive.

Comments: _____

_____

_____

_____

_____

_____

_____

_____

Model D

Score: ▽

Alone on a Deserted Island

The things I would want if I was stranded on a deserted island would be matches, a knife, and a box of plastic trash bags. With these three things, I might survive.

The matchs' main purpose would be to build a fire. A fire would warm me. A fire would help me cook my food I could also use a fire to signal ships and planes.

A knife's main purpose would be to help me make tools and a shelter. Then I could hunt for food and be staying out of the rain and wind.

The plastic trash bag's main purpose is to collect water. I could also use them to keep the shelter dry or to sleep on. If I put them on. They would keep me warm.

I would use these three things to help me survive.

Comments: _____

_____

_____

_____

_____

_____

_____

_____

WRITING AN EXPOSITORY ESSAY

Now you get to write your own expository essay. Use the prompt below.

> *Write an essay about a science experiment or concept that interested or surprised you.*

When You Write Your Expository Essay

1. **Think about** what you want to write. Ask yourself some questions.
   - What is my topic?
   - What are the most important ideas I want to explain about this topic?
   - What details will help make my explanation clear?
   - In what order should I organize my ideas and details?
   - How can I grab my readers' attention at the beginning?
   - How should I bring the essay to a conclusion?

   Use graphic organizers to gather and sort the information.

2. **Write** your first draft. Check that you've organized your writing into a clear beginning, middle, and ending.

3. **Read** your draft. Use the checklist that your teacher will give you to review your writing

4. **Edit** your essay. Make changes until your essay gives a clear explanation of the topic.

5. **Proofread** your essay one last time.

6. **Write** a neat copy of your essay and give it to your partner.

Work with a Partner

7. **Read** your partner's expository essay.

8. **Score** your partner's essay from 1 to 4, using the rubric on page 112. Then complete the Partner Comments sheet that your teacher will give you. Tell what you like about the essay and what you think would make it better.

9. **Switch** papers.

10. **Think about** your partner's comments. Read your essay again. Make changes that you think will improve your expository essay.

11. **Write** a neat final copy of your expository essay.

Making Connections

- Much of the writing in your science and social studies books is expository writing, which explains various topics. Look through these books and notice how the writers have used headings, captions, and special kinds of type to add structure and organization to long chapters.

- Newspapers, magazines, and television guides also provide models of expository writing. Look for articles that explain how or why something happened. Look for "how to" articles and recipes in magazines and newspapers. All of these are explanations.

- News programs and documentaries on TV also give explanations. They are good examples of how expository writing can be entertaining as well as informative.

PERSUASIVE ESSAYS

An opinion is what you think or believe to be true about something. When you write a paper to convince readers to share your opinion, you are writing a persuasive essay.

Here is a sample writing prompt for a persuasive essay.

> *Write an essay presenting your opinion about healthy eating.*

Read the persuasive essay, which was written in response to the prompt. Then read the Writing Tips to learn more about persuasive essays.

Writing Tips

❊ Begin your essay by introducing the topic and your opinion about it. Try to capture your readers' interest by including an interesting fact or example.

❊ Support your opinion with convincing reasons. Use each reason as the main idea of a paragraph. The supporting detail sentences should be relevant, clearly stated facts or examples.

❊ Think of at least one objection that others might have to your opinion, and write a point that argues against it.

❊ Carefully choose precise words to press your case. Avoid statements that seem to be based on emotions or that sound confusing or weak.

❊ Use a tone that sounds confident, but always be polite. You want your readers to agree with you, not get mad at you.

❊ Bring your persuasive essay to an effective conclusion. You may want to save your strongest reason for the end.

You Are What You Eat

My grandmother always used to tell me, "You are what you eat." At first I didn't know what she meant. Then the more I thought about it, the more I began to understand and even agree with her. It's really simple. If you eat a lot healthy food, you'll be healthy. If you eat a lot of junk food, you won't be as healthy.

Everyone knows what junk foods are. They are things like fries, candy, potato chips, and ice cream. The trouble is that junk food tastes so good! That's because it's usually filled with sugar and fat, but sugar and fat aren't good for you. They make you overweight, and that's bad. It's bad for your health because it can lead to diabetes. I know because my cousin has it.

Everyone also knows what healthy foods are. They are things like cereals, fruits, and vegetables. Most people think these foods don't taste too good, but they can taste better than you think. Have your mom put some melted cheese on your broccoli, or put some whipped topping on some fruit. Have you ever tried peanut butter on celery? If you stop and think about it, there really are many ways to make healthy food taste better.

Should you stop eating all junk food? That would be a good idea, but it's probably impossible! What you can do, though, is try to eat more healthy food. Healthy eating will make you look and feel better. You'll also be stronger and healthier.

USING GRAPHIC ORGANIZERS

Before you write, use graphic organizers to gather and organize the arguments for your persuasive essay.

The writer of the persuasive essay on page 116 might have used an Opinion Chart, such as the one below.

What is the topic?
healthy eating

What is your opinion?
You are what you eat.

An Opinion Chart helps writers arrange ideas for persuasive essays.

What reasons, facts, or examples back up your opinion?		
Junk foods add weight that can lead to diabetes.	Healthy food can taste better if you work at it.	Work at eating more healthy food and less junk food if you want to look and feel better.

What objection might someone offer?
Junk food tastes better than good food.

How can you address that argument?
Healthy food can taste good, and you don't have to stop eating *all* junk food.

Another way to organize reasons and for a persuasive essay is with a Reason/Details Web. If you had been the writer of the persuasive essay on page 116, how might you have used this web? Fill in the empty ovals with details about healthy eating.

A Reason/Details Web helps writers organize the reasons that support their opinion.

The Benefits of Healthy Eating

Score: **4**

Read the persuasive essay below, which was written in response to the prompt on page 116. Read the comments and think about why this essay scored a 4.

Healthy Eating Is Common Sense

Which is better for you, a cheeseburger or a turkey sandwich? Everyone know the answer is a turkey sandwich. It's better because it doesn't have so much fat in it, and it has fewer calories.

My opinion is that you don't have to be a rocket scientist to eat in a healthy way. You just have to use your common sense.

Let's start with breakfast. Should you go to school without eating anything? The answer is a big no! Common sense says that everyone needs some fuel to get the body working in the morning. Common sense also says that eating some cereal with fruit is better than eating three donuts. All the sugar in the donuts will give you a big burst of energy, but it won't last very long.

Healthy eating isn't always easy at lunch because you have to eat what the cafeteria serves. If you have any choices, let your common sense guide you. For example, would a carton of 1% milk be better than a soda? You're right. Drink the milk along with your burger.

For dinner let your common sense help you choose not only what you'll eat but also how much of it you'll eat. No one has to tell you, for example, that a good balance isn't for bites of broccoli and a huge dish of chocolate ice cream.

I can hear you saying, "Donuts, soda, and chocolate ice cream taste better than cereal, milk, and broccoli." You're right. You can eat those things. I do. Just use your common sense and balance what you eat. To me, healthy eating is common sense.

Your Turn

Now it's your turn to help the writer. Find and fix the errors in the writing. Go back to the pages in green if you need help.

1. Find and fix the error in **subject-verb agreement.** See pp. 20–21.

2. Find and fix the incorrect **homophone.** See pp. 28–29.

TEACHER COMMENTS

4

▲ Your title gives your position right away. Good!
▲ I like the way you lead into your essay with a direct question.
▲ Your examples and facts support your opinion and are arranged logically in a logical order.
▲ You really do a nice job of varying the types, structures, and lengths of sentences.
▲ Your essay clearly states an objection that someone might raise, and you counter it with a suggestion of your own.
▲ Your essay concludes with a clear statement of your opinion.

PARTNER COMMENTS

3

2

Your essay made a lot of sense to me. Your arguments were strong and convincing.

Read the persuasive essay and the comments that follow. Think about why this essay scored a 3.

Common Sense

I'm no rocket scientist but I know how to eat right. I just use my common sense. I mean, I might prefer to eat a hamburger, but I know that a turkey sandwich would be better for me. I believe that healthy eating is common sense.

I use my common sense about food all day long. My brother eats donuts for breakfast almost every morning. I like donuts too but when I eat them sometimes my energy level crashes around 10 o'clock and then I get really tired. A bowl of cereal and fruit actually makes my energy last longer in the morning.

I have a hard time eating a healthy lunch at school because the school cafeteria serve so much junk food. I still think there are choices. I'm tempted sometimes to get a soda to drink with my lunch. My common sense tells me that a carton of 1% milk is more better for me.

Common sense tells me two things. It tells me what to eat and how much to eat. This always comes up at dinner. I'd much rather skip the broccoli and go for a big bowl of chocolate ice cream for dessert. I usually try to eat more broccoli and a little less ice cream.

Of course, the trouble is that all the stuff that's bad for you tastes so good! I know. I love junk food myself. If I close my eyes right now I can taste that chocolate ice cream! My common sense gets lost sometimes when I'm tempted with things like that, but I still believe that healthy eating is common sense.

Your Turn

Now it's your turn to help the writer. Find and fix the errors in the writing. Go back to the pages in green if you need help.

1. Find and fix the missing **comma** in a **compound sentence**. See pp. 30–31.

2. Find and fix the **rambling sentence**. See pp. 40–41.

3. Find and fix the error in **subject-verb agreement**. See pp. 18–19.

4. Find and fix the **double comparison**. See pp. 22–23.

5. Find and fix the **introductory dependent clause** that is missing a **comma**. See pp. 52–53.

TEACHER COMMENTS

▲ Thank you for stating the topic and your opinion in the first paragraph.

▲ Your reasons for your opinion are clear, and you back them up with some good examples.

▲ Your ending is a little weak because you spend more time on the objection than on your own argument.

▲ You should try **varying** some **sentence beginnings**. See pp. 44–45 for help.

PARTNER COMMENTS

You made a lot of good points about using common sense to eat better, except at the end. Also, you started too many sentences the same way.

Score: **2**

Read the persuasive essay and the comments that follow. Think about why this essay scored a 2.

1

Choices Are Hard

I wish good food tasted good and bad food tasted bad. It's hard to eat right. Most of the good food always taste bad. A turkey sandwich doesn't taste bad, but it doesn't taste nearly as good as a hamburger and fries.

The food at school is usually real bad. What can I do? If there's no good food, I can't eat it. I guess I could drink milk sometimes. Really only like chocolate milk. That's bad too, I guess. Every morning my brother eats donuts for breakfast. They look good. I ate them sometimes when I'm rushing out the door. At other times I eat cereal. It's good, but donuts taste more better.

Well you know what you should eat. The trouble is the taste. Eat it anyway. Sometimes you have to eat bad stuff too. Because it tastes so good!

2

PARTNER COMMENTS

Your opinion wasn't very clear. Your ideas were mixed up so they were hard to follow.

3

Your Turn

Now it's your turn to help the writer. Find and fix the errors in the writing. Go back to the pages in green if you need help.

1. Find and fix the error in **subject-verb agreement**. See pp. 20–21.
2. Find and fix the **adjective** that should be an **adverb**. See pp. 26–27.
3. Find and fix the two **sentence fragments**. See pp. 34–35.
4. Find and fix the **paragraph** that should be **indented**. See pp. 58–59.
5. Find and fix the **inconsistent verb tense**. See pp. 16–17.
6. Find and fix the **double comparison**. See pp. 22–23.
7. Find and fix the **introductory word** that should be followed by a **comma**. See pp. 52–53.

TEACHER COMMENTS

4

▲ Your title doesn't relate specifically to your topic. Try to relate it more to your opinion about eating healthy.

▲ Your reasons for eating in a healthy way need to be stronger, and you need to organize your reasons in a logical and convincing order. Then you need to support each reason with facts and examples.

▲ Use a graphic organizer to plan your essay. Then your ideas will be stronger and less confusing.

▲ Throughout, you seem to agree with the objection argument that bad food tastes good. Instead, you should try to get your readers to agree with your opinion about healthy eating.

▲ You used vague words like *stuff, bad,* and *good.* Your essay would be stronger if you chose more **exact words**. See pp. 4–5 and 22–27 for help.

Read the persuasive essay and the comments that follow. Think about why this essay scored a 1.

I like hamburgers and fries and I know I shouldnt ought to eat them because they are junk food and junk food is bad for you. I could eat a turkey sandwich. Sometimes I do. My brother and me don't always eat breakfast. We should. I no. Sometimes we eat donuts. I also eat cereal and bananas. I don't eat green bananas. Only yellow ones. Bananas aren't junk food, but they taste well. Most good food tastes bad. Does broccoli taste good to you? I bet your answer is no. Thats my answer. I would rather have a big dish of chocolate ice cream, and then have a donut. They is my favorite foods. What are yours? Try to eat good food on principal.

2

PARTNER COMMENTS

Your writing was supposed to give an opinion about healthy eating, but you didn't follow the prompt. In fact, you talked more about unhealthy eating.

3

TEACHER COMMENTS

▲ What is your topic? What is your opinion? You should be giving your opinion about healthy eating.

▲ Organize more of the reasons for your opinion into indented **paragraphs**. Then support each reason with one or two **details.** See pp. 58–59 for help.

▲ Use **transitional words** or **phrases** to connect your ideas. See pp. 60–61.

▲ Use more **exact** and **vivid words** to make your writing more interesting to read. See pp. 4–5 and 22–27.

▲ Try to **join** short **sentences** that have related ideas. See pp. 30–31, 34–39, and 44–45.

Your Turn

Now it's your turn to help the writer. Find and fix the errors in the writing. Go back to the pages in green if you need help.

1. Find and fix the **rambling sentence.** See pp. 40–41.

2. Find and fix the two **contraction** errors. See pp. 54–55.

3. Find and fix the **unnecessary phrase.** See pp. 42–43.

4. Find and fix the incorrect **pronoun.** See pp. 10–11.

5. Find and fix the two incorrect **homophones**. See pp. 28–29.

6. Find and fix the **sentence fragment.** See pp. 34–35.

7. Find and fix the **adverb** that should be an **adjective.** See pp. 26–27.

8. Find and fix the **comma** that is used incorrectly in a **simple sentence** with a **compound predicate.** See pp. 44–45.

9. Find and fix the error in **subject-verb agreement.** See pp. 18–19.

4

This rubric is based on a point scale of 1 to 4. It was used to score the persuasive essays on pages 118–121. Use the rubric to remember what is important in persuasive essays.

4 A score of 4 means that the writer

- ❑ connects the writing directly to the prompt.
- ❑ almost always uses the correct forms of words.
- ❑ almost always uses capitalization and punctuation correctly.
- ❑ almost always uses clear and complete sentences and includes variety in sentences.
- ❑ uses effective words.
- ❑ creates a title that relates to the opinion.
- ❑ creates a clear beginning, middle, and ending.
- ❑ clearly introduces the topic and the opinion in the beginning.
- ❑ backs up the opinion with strong reasons, facts, and examples.
- ❑ presents the ideas in an order that strengthens the opinion.
- ❑ clearly anticipates and addresses at least one objection.
- ❑ begins a new paragraph for each change of idea.

2 A score of 2 means that the writer

- ❑ connects the writing to the prompt in a general way.
- ❑ uses some incorrect forms of words.
- ❑ uses some incorrect capitalization or punctuation.
- ❑ uses little variety in sentences.
- ❑ uses some run-on or rambling sentences or sentence fragments.
- ❑ uses mostly simple words.
- ❑ creates a title.
- ❑ presents a weak a beginning, middle, or ending.
- ❑ presents a weak or confusing opinion.
- ❑ may provide too few reasons, facts, or examples to support the opinion.
- ❑ presents the ideas in an unclear order.
- ❑ weakly anticipates or addresses a possible objection.
- ❑ may make some paragraphing errors.

3 A score of 3 means that the writer

- ❑ connects the writing to the prompt.
- ❑ usually uses the correct forms of words.
- ❑ usually uses capitalization and punctuation correctly.
- ❑ usually uses clear and complete sentences and includes variety in sentences.
- ❑ uses some effective words.
- ❑ creates a title that generally relates to the opinion.
- ❑ creates a beginning, middle, and ending.
- ❑ introduces the topic and the opinion in the beginning.
- ❑ backs up the opinion with some reasons, facts, and examples.
- ❑ presents the ideas in an order that makes sense.
- ❑ anticipates and addresses at least one objection.
- ❑ usually begins a new paragraph for each change of idea.

1 A score of 1 means that the writer

- ❑ does not successfully connect the writing to the prompt.
- ❑ uses many incorrect forms of words.
- ❑ often uses incorrect capitalization or punctuation.
- ❑ uses almost no variety in sentences.
- ❑ uses many run-on or rambling sentences or sentence fragments.
- ❑ uses simple or inappropriate words.
- ❑ creates a poor title or has no title at all.
- ❑ presents an unclear beginning, middle, or ending.
- ❑ may not state the opinion or does not provide enough reasons, facts, or examples to back up the opinion.
- ❑ may include unimportant details.
- ❑ presents the ideas in a confusing order.
- ❑ fails to anticipate or address a possible objection.
- ❑ may make many paragraphing errors.

SCORING PERSUASIVE ESSAYS

Now it's your turn to score some persuasive essays. The four essays on pages 123 and 124 were written in response to this prompt.

> *Write an opener for your school's website, convincing readers to learn more about your school.*

Read each persuasive essay. Write a few comments about it. Then give it a score from 1 to 4. Think about what you've learned in this lesson as you match each essay with its correct score.

Model A

Score: ▽

Our Website

This is our school's website. It shows ourselves really good. Lots of people go on the Internet to find information. Do you want to know about our school? We do science, history, math, and other subjects. In science we learned about parasites and bacteria. Some of them is helpful. In history we learned about the Dust Bowl and the poor farmers who had to move out West and in math we learned how to draw cubes.

Slides, photos, voices, songs, and a demonstration all is found on our website. Click the Science, History, or Math buttons. Other schools teach these subjects to. We think our school is Number 1.

Comments: _____
_____
_____
_____
_____
_____
_____
_____

Model B

Score: ▽

Here's Our School!

Our school is a great school. To learn about things we study and why our school is the best, you can explore our website. Here are some highlights.

If you click the Science button you'll see slides. Bacteria and parasites lives in our bodies. Some of these microscopic animals are helpful. One lives on your face.

Click the History button. You'll see a presentation about the Dust Bowl. That happened in the 1930s. We have photos, voices, and songs of the parched land.

Under the Math button there's a lesson in computer animation.

You may know of other schools that do some of the same things. We do them all. Everyone in our school knows that we are number 1.

Comments: _____
_____
_____
_____
_____
_____
_____

Model C

Score: ▽

Our school's website. Our teachers, our principal, and our school is great. Theres history and math. Theres science too and some little animals live on our bodies, I think there called bacteria. You can see the slides for yourselves. We learned about farmers who were poor in history class in the 1930s. You can draw a cube in math and you put it on the computer and it turns and you can see the cube sides. If you click the buttons you can see lots of stuff. Its our school.

Comments: _____
_____
_____
_____
_____
_____
_____
_____
_____

Model D

Score: ▽

Welcome to Our School Website!

Did you know that critters live in and on your body? Are you aware that the Dust Bowl is not a football game? To get these and other answers, explore our school website. Here are some highlights.

Click the Science button to see slides of bacteria and parasites, and you'll hear students tell about beneficial animals that call our bodies home. For example, there's probably a microscopic spider relative, *demodex folliculorum*, on your face right now!

Click the History button for a Dust Bowl presentation and be transported to the 1930s in Kansas. You'll see photos of parched land and hear the voices and songs of people who migrated West for a chance at a better life.

Do other schools have classes that cover these subjects? Sure they do, but we cover these subjects and much, much more! You must agree that we are Number 1!

Comments: _____
_____
_____
_____
_____
_____
_____
_____

WRITING A PERSUASIVE ESSAY

Now you get to write your own persuasive essay. Use the prompt below.

> *Write a letter nominating a classmate for the Student of the Year award.*

When You Write Your Persuasive Essay

1. **Think about** what you want to write. Ask yourself some questions.
   - What is my opinion?
   - What examples or facts can I use to support my reasons for the opinion?
   - What is the best order in which to present my reasons?
   - How might someone oppose my opinion? How could I argue against the objection?

   Use graphic organizers to gather and sort the information.

2. **Write** your first draft. Build strong arguments to support your opinion.

3. **Read** your draft. Use the checklist that your teacher will give you to review your writing.

4. **Edit** your essay. Make changes until your essay presents a strong argument.

5. **Proofread** your essay one last time.

6. **Write** a neat copy of your essay and give it to your partner.

Work with a Partner

7. **Read** your partner's persuasive essay.

8. **Score** your partner's essay from 1 to 4, using the rubric on page 122. Then complete the Partner Comments sheet that your teacher will give you. Tell what you like about the essay and what you think would make it better.

9. **Switch** papers.

10. **Think about** your partner's comments. Read your essay again. Make changes that you think will improve your persuasive essay.

11. **Write** a neat final copy of your persuasive essay.

Making Connections

- Examine examples of persuasive writing in your world. Read letters to the editor, advertisements, brochures, and movie reviews. Think about the kinds of supporting details the writers use. Decide which are the most effective and why.

- Think about the last time that someone changed your mind about something important. Consider why the person's arguments were effective with you and whether or not they would be effective with other people.

- Think about your opinions. In your journal, make a two-column chart. On one side, list topics about which you have strong opinions. On the other side, list some reasons for your opinions. Check off the reasons that might persuade someone else to agree with you and then cross out weaker arguments, such as "All my friends think so."

Summarizing is one way to show that you understand what you read. A summary briefly restates the most important points of a longer piece of writing. For a summary of fiction, you briefly present the characters and events. For a summary of nonfiction, you briefly state the main ideas and essential details in your own words.

Here is a sample writing prompt for a summary of a nonfiction article.

> *Read the article "Bats!" on page 127. Then write a summary of the article.*

Read the article on page 127 and read the summary below, which was written in response to the prompt. Then read the Writing Tips to learn more about summaries.

Writing Tips

* At the beginning of the summary, mention the topic of the article. Then paraphrase, or restate in your own words, the article's main ideas and any essential supporting details.

* Headings printed in bold type in the article can help you identify important ideas.

* Because your summary should be just one paragraph long, be concise.

* Arrange the ideas in the order in which the author presents them in the main article.

* Keep the summary simple. Avoid colorful language unless it relates to the article.

* Use your own words whenever possible. It's all right to quote key words, facts, or details from the article. Do not copy long passages from the article, though.

* Never add to a summary any ideas or opinions that are not contained in the original article. Stick to what the author wrote.

Bats are furry mammals with five long fingers that form the support for their wings. Bats can fly because the curved shape of their wings allows lift. Bats come out at night to eat. They eat fruit, flowers, and insects. Most bats can eat up to 1,000 mosquitoes an hour. This ability makes them a valuable insect-control resource. One kind of bat, the vampire bat, drinks, not sucks, blood. Though feared and misunderstood, bats are amazing animals.

BATS!

Bats are mammals with furry bodies. They roost in dark places such as caves, attics, and trees, and they only come out at night to eat.

Mammals with Wings

A bat is like a flying mouse, with similar body components even down to the five fingers on its hands. On a bat, however, the fingers are extremely long. These fingers form the skeletal support for the wings. Unlike birds, whose wings are covered with feathers, a bat's wings are covered only by two thin layers of skin controlled by flexible muscles.

Bats are the only true flying mammals. Flying squirrels and flying lemurs merely glide downward. Bats, like birds, can rise and swoop and then soar skyward once again. How can they do this? Their thin wings are curved like the wings of an aircraft. The curve provides lift, which allows bats to fly.

Bug Zappers

To people, a mosquito might signal a threat. To a bat, a mosquito signals food. Although many bat species eat fruits or flowers, others eat meat. For many bats in the temperate zone, insects are the food of choice. With superb echolocation abilities, a bat can identify a mosquito at a distance and catch it in flight. A single bat can eat more than 1,000 mosquitoes each hour. That's why bats are a major insect-control resource for human communities.

Vampire Bats

As rumored, there are bats that feed on blood. The vampire bat, located only in the tropics, makes a tiny cut in a victim and then laps, not sucks, the blood that runs out. These bats usually bite horses, cattle, and other warm-blooded animals. Although they have been known to bite humans, their bite doesn't kill. They can spread disease, though.

Bats, though sometimes feared and misunderstood, are nonetheless amazing animals and superior insect-control specialists.

USING GRAPHIC ORGANIZERS

Before you write, use graphic organizers to sort and arrange the main ideas and details to include in your summary.

The writer of the summary on page 126 might have used a Topic Web, such as the one below.

A Topic Web helps writers sort out the main ideas from a longer passage.

```
   Bug Zappers          Flying Mammals
                          with Wings

              BATS


          Vampire Bats
```

A Main Ideas/Details Chart also helps writers summarize the most important ideas in a nonfiction article. If you had been the writer of the summary on page 126, how would you have used the chart below? Fill in main ideas and details from the article on page 127.

A Main Ideas/Details Chart helps writers summarize important ideas.

```
                    BATS


  Main Idea:        Main Idea:         Main Idea:
  _____     _____      _____

  Details:          Details:           Details:

  _____     _____      _____
  _____     _____      _____
  _____     _____      _____
```

Score:

Read the summary below, which was written in response to the prompt on page 126. Read the comments and think about why this summary scored a 4.

1

Bats are mammals that fly. They are able to fly because their wings are shaped in a way that gives them lift. A bats extremely long fingers form a supporting skeleton for its wings. Bats, which feed at night, eat mostly fruits, flowers, and insects. Most bats eat insects in huge quantities. In doing so, they help control the insect population for humans. One bat, the vampire bat, actually feeds on blood. Bats are often feared and misunderstood but they are nonetheless amazing.

2

Your Turn

Now it's your turn to help the writer. Find and fix the errors in the writing. Go back to the pages in green if you need help.

1. Find and fix the incorrect **possessive noun**. See pp. 8–9.

2. Find and fix the **compound sentence** that is missing a **comma**. See pp. 30–31.

PARTNER COMMENTS

Your summary included all the main ideas from the article. Reading this summary helped me focus on the most important points in the article.

3

TEACHER COMMENTS

4

▲ Your summary paraphrases all the author's key points and includes only necessary details. Nice job!

▲ Other than necessary key terms, you use your own words to summarize. It is clear that you understand what you have read.

▲ I appreciate the fact that you follow the order of the ideas in the article and that you use some transitional words to connect the ideas.

▲ Thank you for not adding new ideas or opinions and for keeping this summary strictly about the article.

▲ You do a nice job of arranging the ideas in a single paragraph.

Read the summary and the comments that follow. Think about why this summary scored a 3.

Score:

1

Bats are mammals, like people. Unlike people, however, bats can fly. Bats have wings that are curved like an airplanes wings. A bat's wings give it lift. A bat has real long fingers. These here fingers form a skeleton for the wings. Different bats feed on different things. Some bats eat thousands of insects but vampire bats lap blood. Even if some bats are scary, all of them is very interesting.

Your Turn

Now it's your turn to help the writer. Find and fix the errors in the writing. Go back to the pages in green if you need help.

1. Find and fix the incorrect **possessive noun.** See pp. 8–9.

2. Find and fix the **adjective** that should be an **adverb.** See pp. 26–27.

3. Find and fix the **unnecessary word.** See pp. 42–43.

4. Find and fix the **compound sentence** that is missing a **comma.** See pp. 30–31.

5. Find and fix the error in **subject-verb agreement.** See pp. 20–21.

2

PARTNER COMMENTS

You included all the author's main ideas in your summary, but you also added some new information about people being mammals. Otherwise, it was a good summary of the article.

3

TEACHER COMMENTS

4

▲ You follow the prompt and introduce the topic of the article right away.

▲ You do a good job of putting the ideas in the same order as they are in the article.

▲ Your word choice is clear. You have not added any colorful language that would distract from the summary.

▲ You include most of the important information from the article, but you add some extra information about people being mammals.

Read the summary and the comments that follow.
Think about why this summary scored a 2.

1

Bats are mammals with furry bodies. They roost in dark places such as caves, attics, and trees, and they only come out at night to eat. Flying squirrels and other flying things glide. Bats curve there wings. Bats have five fingers. Bats have long fingers a bats fingers are on its wings. John my next-door neighbor and me don't like flying bugs. Bats like them. They eat them. Some bats eat blood. Thats worst. Bats eat tons of bugs each night.

2

Your Turn

Now it's your turn to help the writer. Find and fix the errors in the writing. Go back to the pages in green if you need help.

1. Find and fix the incorrect **homophone**. See pp. 28–29.

2. Find and fix the **run-on sentence**. See pp. 40–41.

3. Find and fix the incorrect **possessive noun**. See pp. 8–9.

4. Find and fix the **appositive phrase** that should be set off by **commas**. See pp. 38–39.

5. Find and fix the incorrect **pronoun**. See pp. 10–11.

6. Find and fix the **contraction** error. See pp. 54–55.

7. Find and fix the incorrect **comparative** form of an **adjective**. See pp. 22–23.

TEACHER COMMENTS

4

▲ The first two sentences of your summary are copied directly from the article. Please use your own words to paraphrase ideas. Don't copy.

▲ Report facts and ideas from the article without adding your own opinions.

▲ Check that ideas are complete and accurate.

▲ Use the article headings to organize your ideas. Write one sentence about each main idea.

▲ Try to **join sentences** that are related to give your writing variety. See pp. 30–31, 34–39, and 44–45 for help.

▲ Try using some **pronouns** instead of using the noun *bats* over and over. See pp. 10–15.

PARTNER COMMENTS

3

It looks like you copied a lot of the writer's words, and you included your own opinions. You also didn't follow the order of the main ideas in the article.

Score:

Read the summary and the comments that follow. Think about why this summary scored a 1.

1

I have seen bats before I read this. I am not afraid of them. Tanya my only sister is. We watched TV, and we saw a program and it was about vampire bats. A vampire bat makes a tiny cut in its victim. Then it laps up the blood that runs out. Birds fly, but they have feathers. Not bats. Some bats eat bugs. Thats good. They won't bite me then. Bats have hands. Bats hands have five fingers. They is like the hands on mice. Bat fingers are longest than mice fingers. I almost forgot bats are mammals.

PARTNER COMMENTS

2

I had a really hard time telling that this was a summary. You copied a little and also added your own opinions. You made too many errors.

TEACHER COMMENTS

3

▲ This summary should only have information from the original article. You've included other information.
▲ To help yourself identify main ideas, write the article headings in a graphic organizer.
▲ It's OK to use important terms from the article, but you should not copy whole phrases or sentences.
▲ Make sure your facts are complete and accurate.
▲ Try to choose words that express the writer's most important ideas.
▲ Use a **pronoun** to replace the word bats sometimes. See pp. 10–15 for help.

2

Your Turn

Now it's your turn to help the writer. Find and fix the errors in the writing. Go back to the pages in green if you need help.

1. Find and fix the error in **past-perfect tense**. See pp. 16–17.

2. Find and fix the **appositive phrase** that should be set off by **commas**. See pp. 38–39.

3. Find and fix the **rambling sentence**. See pp. 40–41.

4. Find and fix the **sentence fragment**. See pp. 34–35.

5. Find and fix the **contraction** error. See pp. 54–55.

6. Find and fix the incorrect **possessive noun**. See pp. 8–9.

7. Find and fix the error in **subject-verb agreement**. See pp. 18–19.

8. Find and fix the incorrect **comparative** form of an **adjective**. See pp. 22–23.

9. Find and fix the **unnecessary words**. See pp. 42–43.

USING A RUBRIC TO SCORE SUMMARIES

This rubric is based on a point scale of 1 to 4. It was used to score the summaries on pages 129–132. Use the rubric to remember what is important in summaries.

4 — A score of 4 means that the writer

- ❏ connects the writing directly to the prompt.
- ❏ almost always uses the correct forms of words.
- ❏ almost always uses capitalization and punctuation correctly.
- ❏ almost always uses clear and complete sentences and includes appropriate variety in sentences.
- ❏ uses effective words.
- ❏ presents the topic at the beginning of the summary.
- ❏ includes only the most important ideas and necessary supporting details from the main article.
- ❏ does not add new information or opinions.
- ❏ uses his or her own words effectively and includes only necessary key terms from the article.
- ❏ presents ideas in the same order as they appear in the article.

2 — A score of 2 means that the writer

- ❏ connects the writing to the prompt in a general way.
- ❏ uses some incorrect forms of words.
- ❏ uses some incorrect capitalization or punctuation.
- ❏ uses little variety in sentences.
- ❏ uses some run-on or rambling sentences or sentence fragments.
- ❏ uses mostly simple words.
- ❏ may not clearly present the topic.
- ❏ includes some important ideas from the main article but may also include unimportant ideas or details.
- ❏ may add new information or opinions or may copy text from the article.
- ❏ uses his or her own words, but they may not reflect the ideas in the article.
- ❏ presents some ideas that do not follow the order of the ideas in the article.

3 — A score of 3 means that the writer

- ❏ connects the writing to the prompt.
- ❏ usually uses the correct forms of words.
- ❏ usually uses capitalization and punctuation correctly.
- ❏ usually uses clear and complete sentences and includes some appropriate variety in sentences.
- ❏ uses some effective words.
- ❏ presents the topic toward the beginning of the summary.
- ❏ includes many important ideas and details from the main article.
- ❏ may add some new information or opinions.
- ❏ uses his or her own words and includes some key terms from the article.
- ❏ presents all or most ideas in the same order as they appear in the article.

1 — A score of 1 means that the writer

- ❏ does not successfully connect the writing to the prompt.
- ❏ uses many incorrect forms of words.
- ❏ often uses incorrect capitalization or punctuation.
- ❏ uses almost no variety in sentences.
- ❏ uses many run-on or rambling sentences or sentence fragments.
- ❏ uses simple or inappropriate words.
- ❏ may not state the topic.
- ❏ includes only a few important ideas from the article.
- ❏ often adds new information or opinions and may copy text from the article.
- ❏ may use his or her own words, but they often don't reflect the ideas in the article.
- ❏ presents many ideas that do not follow the order of the ideas in the article.

SCORING SUMMARIES

Now it's your turn to score some summaries. The four summaries on this page were written in response to this prompt.

Read the passage "What Is a Rainforest?" on page 135. Then write a summary of it.

Read each summary below. Write a few comments about it. Then give it a score from 1 to 4. Think about what you've learned in this lesson as you match each summary with its correct score.

Model A

Score:

A rainforest is a hot, sunny, rainy place. The tropics get about 6 to 8 hours of sunlight each day. Very little rain and sunlight gets to the floor. Thats where insects help make humus for seeds to grow. The trees grow real tall. Plants grow on them to reach the sun and rain.

*Comments:*_____

_____

_____

_____

Model C

Score:

Each day a tropical rainforest has about the same amount of sunlight, about an 80°F temperature, and some rainfall. Because very little sunlight and rainfall reach the rainforest floor, most plants grow in the canopy. Trees and other plants seek sunlight and rain there. Rainforests are a diverse environment.

*Comments:*_____

_____

_____

Model B

Score:

I have been to Oregon. Oregons forests are beautiful. Rainy to. Just like rainforests. Rains every day there. Its hot and its humid and there are sun and clouds. Lots of animals and plants and trees lives there. There are them there masses of orchids, squawking parrots, and groups of monkeys to. In the canopy. Seeds grow on the floor.

*Comments:*_____

_____

_____

Model D

Score:

A rainforest is a real hot place. Tropical rainforests also have high humidity levels that changes little from season to season. It also rains a lot. Its sunny to because of the Equator. The rainforest has a floor and a canopy. Plants and animals lives in the canopy. Not so many on the floor, though.

*Comments:*_____

_____

_____

_____

Here is the article from which the summaries on page 134 were written.

WHAT IS A RAINFOREST?

Three qualities distinguish rainforests from other woodlands: constant levels of sunlight, a high average temperature, and almost daily rainfall.

Rainforest Climate

Unlike their more northern or southern neighboring forests, tropical rainforests do not suffer from seasonal extremes of heat and cold or drought and rain. Positioned on or near the equator, the angle of the earth's tilt helps give the tropical rainforest a steady stream of sunlight and an average temperature of about 80°F. High humidity levels build clouds, which protect the land from baking into a desert, while providing regular rainfall. A rainforest typically accumulates from 70 to 100 inches of rain per year.

The Rainforest Floor

With all that rain and sunshine, you might expect a veritable garden on the floor of a tropical rainforest. If you did, you'd be disappointed. Only 10% of the rain and 1% of the sunlight ever make it to the forest floor. As a result, hundreds of species of insects turn debris from fallen leaves into humus, which enriches the soil. Sprouting from this soil are the seeds for trees. These might eventually grow to form the forest canopy, or top leafy layer. The seeds' only chance for survival, however, is if a taller tree dies or falls in a storm. Then a temporary opening in the canopy allows rainfall and sunlight to flood the forest floor. Saplings shoot up and fight for their time in the sun.

The Rainforest Canopy

If you associate masses of orchids, squawking parrots, and groups of monkeys with the rainforest, you'll have to look way, way up to see them. The canopy of the rainforest can stretch more than 120 feet above you. Over thousands of years, trees have tried to top each other in an attempt to capture sunlight and rainfall. Other plants sought their share by creeping up tree trunks and making their homes in the branches in the canopy. Dense masses of leaves and plant roots in the canopy develop pockets that catch dead leaves, which decompose into humus. Flower seeds dropped into this soil take root to create "rooftop" gardens.

Millions of species of plants, animals, and insects have adapted to this steady diet of sunshine, rain, and heat. As a result, rainforests have become the most biologically diverse environment in the world.

WRITING A SUMMARY

Now you get to write your own summary. Use the prompt below.

Read the article "Our Naturalist President: Theodore Roosevelt" on page 137. Then write a summary of it.

When You Write Your Summary

1. **Think about** what you want to write. Ask yourself some questions.
   - What is the topic of the article?
   - How can I use the headings to select and organize ideas for a summary?
   - What are the main ideas of the article?
   - Are there any important words that I need to include or define?

   Use graphic organizers to gather and sort the information.

2. **Write** your first draft. Remember that a summary should be brief. Try to write one or two sentences for each main idea.

3. **Read** your draft. Use the checklist that your teacher will give you to review your writing.

4. **Edit** your summary. Make sure the main ideas are concisely stated and are in the same order as they appear in the original article.

5. **Proofread** your summary one last time.

6. **Write** a neat copy of your summary and give it to your partner.

Work with a Partner

7. **Read** your partner's summary.

8. **Score** your partner's summary from 1 to 4, using the rubric on page 133. Then complete the Partner Comments sheet that your teacher will give you. Tell what you like about the summary and what you think would make it better.

9. **Switch** papers.

10. **Think about** your partner's comments. Read your summary again. Make changes that you think will improve your summary.

11. **Write** a neat final copy of your summary.

Making Connections

- Think about a television show or movie that you have seen recently. How would you summarize the plot for a friend? Think about the most important ideas about the characters and events and how you would describe them in about five sentences.

- Find a book that you have already read and think about how you would summarize it. Then read the summary on the back of the book or on the book jacket. Compare your summary with the printed one.

- A teacher may ask you to summarize an article from a science or social studies book as a homework assignment. Look at the headings that organize the main points of the article. Use the headings and the topic sentences of each paragraph to help you organize your summary.

Read this passage. Then follow the prompt on page 136 for writing a summary.

OUR NATURALIST PRESIDENT: THEODORE ROOSEVELT

Two and a half months after becoming America's twenty-sixth President, Theodore Roosevelt, or TR as he was called, set forth his first address to Congress. In it, he presented a new agenda that he had for the presidency and the country—the conservation of our nation's natural resources.

TR's First Address to Congress

To President Roosevelt, the government had a solemn duty to protect America's natural heritage of plants, animals, water, and land against wasteful and selfish practices. He demanded that the Bureau of Forestry be the single authority controlling the nation's forest reserves. He wanted increased presidential power to set aside more forestlands. He argued for a federal irrigation program to increase the farmland. TR was convinced that the country was at a crossroads. Americans were using more resources faster than at any previous time in history. If the leaders of the nation did not act soon, America's abundant natural resources would be squandered.

TR, the Outdoorsman

TR's commitment to the conservation of our natural resources was rooted in his passionate love of the outdoors. Strenuous exercises such as hiking, rowing, and rock climbing were a normal part of his routine. Even as president, TR found peace when camping outdoors. During one trip in Yosemite, his guide  was the famous conservationist and founder of the Sierra Club, John Muir. Roosevelt's visits with Muir to the Grand Canyon, the Rainbow Bridge, and the gigantic sequoia trees of the California coast helped strengthen TR's resolve to protect the environment and the national parks.

TR's Legacy

Many Americans associate Theodore Roosevelt with the building of the Panama Canal. This achievement was only a part of TR's legacy. In addition, Roosevelt created 5 national parks. He preserved the Grand Canyon against future mining by giving it the status of a national monument. He saved 15 other wilderness areas, such as Muir Woods in California, by declaring them to be national monuments as well. He established 16 federal bird refuges, including Pelican Island in Florida.

Mostly, President Theodore Roosevelt educated the legislature, the public, and the business world to understand that it was in America's best interest to take care of the country's wilderness areas.

When you have a test prompt for expository writing, you usually can rely on facts, examples, and reasons that you already know. In class, however, you may be asked to write **research reports** about real people, places, or things. For these, you will need to supplement what you already know with information from other sources.

TOPIC

When you are assigned a research report, you might be given an exact topic, or you might be given a general topic that you have to narrow. For example, you would need to narrow this topic to make it more manageable: *Explain the causes of a disaster in nature.*

You can narrow this topic by focusing on a particular type of disaster. Do you want to research storms? Climate extremes? Oil spills? Forest fires?

If you decide to focus on forest fires, use what you already know to pose questions about possible causes. Does nature cause forest fires? Do humans cause forest fires? Are forest fires ever set on purpose?

SOURCES

Once you've narrowed your topic and have identified some questions to research, prepare to search out the information for your report. Some **sources** you might use at home or in the library include: nonfiction books, encyclopedias, researched magazine articles, and the Internet.

NOTES

As you read your sources, take **notes** to help yourself remember the most important information that you find. For example, you might write the notes in your notebook or on index cards.

As you take notes, begin making a **bibliography**, a list of your sources. List information such as the title, author, date of publication, publisher, city and state, volume, and the pages you used. If you used a website, list the Internet address. You may be asked to submit your bibliography along with your report.

ORGANIZATION

One way to begin to arrange your notes for writing your report is to use a **graphic organizer**. There are many kinds of graphic organizers. Since this report is to be organized around the causes of one effect (forest fires), you could use a **Cause/Effect Diagram**, such as the one below. Notice that there are 3 causes and 1 effect.

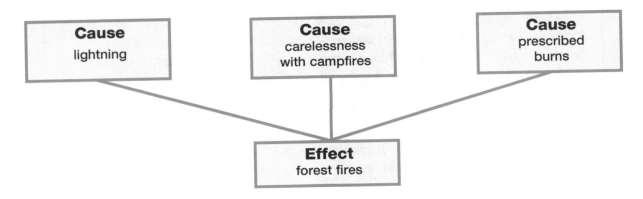

Cause
lightning

Cause
carelessness
with campfires

Cause
prescribed
burns

Effect
forest fires

Once you have completed a graphic organizer, you can add details that you have gathered to create an outline. Then you should use the outline to write the body of your report. Begin the outline by stating the report topic at the top. For the outline for this report, you might list each cause of forest fires as a main idea and then provide details that tell about each cause. Use the report on page 140 to complete the outline below.

Causes of Forest Fires

I. **Cause 1: Lightning**

    A. summer drought _____

    B. _____

    C. _____

II. **Cause 2: Carelessness with Campfires**

    A. _____

    B. _____

        1. _____

        2. _____

        3. _____

III. **Cause 3: Prescribed Burns**

    A. _____

    B. _____

    C. _____

In addition to ideas and details from the outline, your report should include an **opening paragraph**, or *introduction*, and a **closing paragraph**, or *conclusion*. Your final report should follow this format.

Beginning   A strong title and an opening paragraph that introduces the topic and grabs readers' attention with a lead.

Middle   Main ideas and supporting details that build the body of the report, using information listed on the outline. Each main idea should have its own paragraph.

Ending   A closing paragraph that sums up the ideas in the report, restates the topic in different words, or gives an overview of the report. It should provide a sense of closure for readers.

Here is a research report that describes three causes of one effect: forest fires. The writer used the outline on page 139 to write a draft. Then the writer edited and proofread the report. The final report scored a 4. It will be published in a class book.

Three Main Causes of Forest Fires

Beginning

All fires need three things in order to burn: oxygen, fuel, and heat. Oxygen is available in the air. In a forest, fuel is also plentiful. Fallen logs, branches, resins in trees, dead leaves, grasses, and pine needles littering the forest floor can burst into flame with one spark. Where does this spark, or heat, come from? It might come from lightning or careless campers. It might even be set on purpose as part of a forester's management plan.

Middle

During a summer drought, the chance of forest fires increases. That's because summer storms bring a lot of lightning but little rain. Lightning hitting a pine during a drought can be the beginning of a catastrophe. Pines are filled with resin, which burns easily. A lightning strike may not cause an immediate fire in a tree. But its spark could ignite dry pine needles on the forest floor. This surface fire could simmer and then ignite a dried-out tree. That tree could send off burning pieces that ignite other trees.

The most difficult forest fires to put out, ground fires, are often caused by careless campers. To put out a campfire, campers often cover it with dirt. This smothering deprives the fire of oxygen. Campers, however, must wait to make sure that the ground is cool to the touch and all remaining coals have been extinguished. If they leave the site too soon, an underground fire can smolder as an undetected "sleeper." This can spread along the shallow roots of nearby trees until it encounters sufficient fuel, such as the core of a drought-stricken pine. The smoldering embers then ignite the tree like a torch, setting off a blaze that could have been prevented.

Blazes are occasionally set for specific reasons. When too much debris builds up on the forest floor, foresters become concerned. This debris is abundant fuel, waiting for a fire to happen. Should the foresters wait for the lightning to strike and the fire to start? Should they step in and prevent the fire by eliminating the source of fuel? Foresters know that once-burned forests don't reburn. If foresters burn an area ahead of time, they can prevent the spread of a future fire. Sometimes the best way to prevent a huge, out-of-control fire is to manage smaller fires. These managed fires are called *prescribed fires*.

Ending

Although any forest fire may become disastrous, forests do eventually grow back. We can all, however, do our best to make sure that preventable fires never happen. You **can** prevent forest fires.

On pages 141–143 are some writing prompts that you might find on a test. Follow each prompt and use the tips provided.

Prompt 1: Write an essay describing a favorite character in a book, movie, or TV show.

Tips

▲ Read the prompt carefully.

▲ Think about the character you plan to describe. How does the character look, talk, and behave? Does the character have any unique features or characteristics?

▲ Plan an essay that is at least three paragraphs long.

▲ Use a logical order of organization.

▲ At the beginning of the essay, tell who you are describing.

▲ Use effective details and sensory words.

▲ Remember that you can use a graphic organizer.

▲ Use comparisons (similes and metaphors) if they strengthen the imagery.

▲ Read your essay to make sure it paints a powerful picture of the character.

▲ Check your writing to correct any errors in capitalization, punctuation, word use, and paragraphing. Also make sure you have written complete and varied sentences.

Prompt 2: Write a story about a time when you faced a challenge in your life.

Tips

▲ Read the prompt carefully.

▲ Make sure the story is about something that happened in your own life. Use the pronouns *I*, *me*, *we*, and *us*.

▲ Think about the story's main events. How do you feel about them? How do you want to present them? Remember that you can use a graphic organizer.

▲ Think about when and where the story will be set.

▲ Decide who else, besides you, will be the people in the story.

▲ Plan a clear beginning, middle, and ending. Use transitional words such as *before*, *then*, and *later* as needed for clarity.

▲ Include interesting story details and use variety in your sentences.

▲ Begin a new paragraph for each new idea or piece of dialogue.

▲ Think of an attention-getting title that relates to the story.

▲ Read through the story to make sure it is clear and easy to read.

▲ Check your story for correct capitalization, punctuation, and word use.

Prompt 3: Write a fictional story about a character who makes a surprising discovery.

Tips

▲ Read the prompt carefully.

▲ Decide when and where the story takes place.

▲ Decide on the main character and the other characters in the story.

▲ Plan the story events. What problem or challenge will the characters face? What will the turning point and the resolution be?

▲ Plan a clear beginning, middle, and ending for the story. Remember that you can use a graphic organizer.

▲ Use interesting words and sentence variety.

▲ If the story includes dialogue, make sure it sounds realistic. Begin a new paragraph for each change of speaker.

▲ Make sure the "voice" of the story is consistent throughout.

▲ Read through your story to make sure it creates the effect that you intend.

▲ Check the story to correct any errors in capitalization, punctuation, and word use.

Prompt 4: Write an essay explaining ways to be helpful at home.

Tips

▲ Read the prompt carefully.

▲ Remember that the main purpose of the essay is to explain.

▲ Plan an essay that is at least three paragraphs long.

▲ What main ideas will you include? How many ways of helping will you cover? What facts, examples, and reasons will you use to back up the main ideas?

▲ Think of an introductory paragraph that tells what the essay is about and makes readers want to know more.

▲ Present the ideas in a logical order, using appropriate transitional words and phrases.

▲ Write a strong ending paragraph that ties up the points in your essay.

▲ Think of a title that will get the readers' attention.

▲ Check the essay to correct any errors in capitalization, punctuation, and word use.

Prompt 5: Write a persuasive essay about something that should change at your school.

Tips

▲ Read the prompt carefully.

▲ Think through the main points of your opinion. Present your opinion at the beginning of the essay. Remember that you can use a graphic organizer.

▲ Base your arguments on what you know from your own experiences and from your reading.

▲ Use convincing reasons, facts, and examples to support your opinion. Stick to what can be proved.

▲ Mention at least one point that others might use to challenge your argument and briefly explain why that opposing view is unconvincing.

▲ Use a confident tone that will encourage readers to agree with you.

▲ Write a strong conclusion, perhaps saving your strongest point for last.

▲ Read through your essay to make sure it presents and supports your position convincingly.

▲ Check your essay to correct any errors in capitalization, punctuation, and word use. Also make sure you have good sentence variety.

Prompt 6: Write a summary of the article "Antarctica" on page 144.

Tips

▲ Read the prompt carefully.

▲ Read the article on page 144, thinking about its main ideas.

▲ Remember that you can use a graphic organizer.

▲ Mention the topic of the article at the beginning of the summary.

▲ Then paraphrase the article's main ideas and any essential supporting details.

▲ Arrange the ideas in the order in which they appear in the article.

▲ Keep your summary short and simple; make it one paragraph long.

▲ Use your own words. You can quote key words, facts, or details, but don't quote long passages from the article.

▲ Make sure you don't add any ideas or opinions of your own.

▲ Read through the summary to make sure that it clearly sums up the article.

▲ Check the summary to correct any errors in capitalization, punctuation, and word use.

Read this article. Then follow the prompt on page 143 for writing a summary.

ANTARCTICA

Antarctica has only recently been explored by scientists.

The Land   Did you know that 90 percent of Earth's ice is concentrated at Antarctica? Antarctica is the continent that encircles the South Pole. Its area is larger than the combined areas of the United States and Mexico. Yet, Antarctica has only recently been explored by scientists, who are eager to learn more about this land and its creatures.

The Climate   In Antarctica, the sun sets only once each year. For 6 months, the sun is visible just above the horizon 24 hours a day. The sun never rises directly overhead to provide midday warmth. Except for brief periods, the sun's weak radiation is not enough to make up for the heat lost during this long winter period. The average winter temperature on Antarctica is about -76°F. Even on a good summer day, the temperature may rise only to about -22°F. This is about the temperature of Barrow, Alaska, in midwinter. Lack of sunlight and severe cold make Antarctica a harsh environment.

The Animals   Because of the severe winter weather, few animals live year-round on the land of Antarctica. Most spend the winter elsewhere, or they live in the ocean. Unlike the barren land of Antarctica, the Southern Ocean around Antarctica teems with life. Krill, tiny shrimp-like creatures, and other plankton thrive in these oxygen-rich waters. These tiny plants and animals make up the heart of Antarctica's food chain.

Whales, penguins, seals, and seabirds feast on krill. In fact, the blue whale, the largest creature on Earth, eats only krill. Other whales, such as southern right whales, humpbacks, minkes, sperm whales, and killer whales, migrate to Antarctic waters each summer. There they fatten up on tons of krill before beginning their northerly winter migrations.

Penguins, petrels, albatrosses, and other birds also call Antarctica home. Six species of seals, including the crabeater, live there as well. Crabeater seals, which actually feed on krill (not on crabs), are some of the most numerous mammals on Earth.

Antarctica may be forbidding, but scientists are finding that this is a unique land that is home to many fascinating creatures.